THE MAN

FROM OXBOW

THE MAN

FROM OXBOW

The Best of Ralph Allen

Edited and with an Introduction by

Christina McCall Newman

McClelland and Stewart Limited, Toronto/Montreal

The Canadian Publishers
McClelland and Stewart Limited
25 Hollinger Road, Toronto 16
PRINTED AND BOUND IN CANADA

CONTENTS

When Ralph Allen died in a Toronto hospital very early in the morning of December 2, 1966, he was fifty-three years old, a good man in the prime of a good life.

Although he had been dangerously ill for more than two months, his doctors thought he had won his struggle with cancer and it was said that he would be back at his desk at the *Toronto Daily Star* shortly after the turn of the New Year. Partly because of this, and partly because in nearly forty years as a reporter and editor, he had shown himself to be such a vital and indomitable man, his death was unexpected and shocking. As news of it was broadcast on radio, printed in newspapers and related over telephones that Friday, scores of people across this country who reckoned themselves among his friends felt the terror of real grief.

A great many of these friends were in one branch or another of the communications business and some of them sat down in front of typewriters, or microphones or television cameras in an attempt to give voice to their outrage at the senselessness of his death and to their wonder at the meaningfulness of his life.

There were, in fact, so many heartfelt public tributes paid to Ralph that it must have been bewildering to people who had not known him. A friend of my husband's, a young politician who is intelligent and literate, phoned him and said, "Look, before yesterday, I'd barely heard the name Ralph Allen. And yet suddenly I feel as though I've been cheated out of knowing a great man."

For Ralph, although he was much talked of and much revered within the precincts of his craft, could hardly have been called celebrated, even in the narrow sense that Canadians reckon celebrity. And no bare recital of what he had done in his life—how he had left the small prairie town of Oxbow, Saskatchewan at sixteen to become a sports writer on *The Winnipeg Tribune,* then a war correspondent for the Toronto *Globe and Mail,* then a novelist and historian and the editor of Canada's most influential magazine, *Maclean's,* and finally, in the last two years of his life, managing editor of the country's biggest newspaper, the *Toronto*

Daily Star—could really explain the personal sense of loss that his death evoked in so many disparate people.

Some men came close, though, to expressing this loss and one who for me came closer than most was Ken Lefolii, a writer who had worked for Ralph Allen on *Maclean's* and was one of his successors as its editor, when he said on the CBC that "a man of singular *style* has died and there is no way to replace the pleasure of his company."

Just what that style was – even after months of thinking and talking about it to Ralph's relatives and friends – is not easy to define. Ralph was a complex as well as an accomplished man. He was a brilliant and very brave reporter; he was an editor of such compelling strength and honesty that nearly everybody who ever worked for him trusted him completely. He was a patriot who despised jingoism, a humanist who loved to go to war. He was a very funny man, a *raconteur* of great talent, a man who could make other men remember for a lifetime the open pleasure they had known with him over bridge tables and at poker games, in fishing camps, on golf courses and at race tracks. He loved to gamble; he ate and drank with gusto. He read omnivorously and remembered what he had read; he could quote Shakespeare and Sam Johnson, Izaak Walton and Edna St. Vincent Millay. Despite the places he had been, the honours he had won, the money he had made, and the tastes he had cultivated, he was never sleek or smug or sophisticated. He hated pretension of any kind and always refused to own property. He won an O.B.E. for his war reporting and yet when this honour was mentioned to him, he would redden with irritation and say, "Hell, so did everybody else." At the end of his life when he had already earned what he called real money from a couple of best-selling books and was making $40,000 a year from his job, he still lived in a rented duplex. He remained forever the man from Oxbow.

Now all these things are true, but they do not add up to any ultimate truth about Ralph. They do not for instance indicate that he was burdened with the most Presbyterian of consciences, that he felt *responsible* to every human being he met, that without being in the least religious (he once described himself as a lapsed Unitarian), he had a firmer hold on the Christian ethic than anyone else I have known.

They do not indicate either that despite his occasional gaiety and his ready wit, he was an introvert who had periods when he was so uncommunicative that he could sit over lunch with a friend

2

like Trent Frayne, a writer he had known for thirty years, and not utter more than half a dozen cranky sentences. Or that he tended, as another friend, the political columnist Charles Lynch, once wrote in a phrase that has been repeated to me in many ways by many friends, "always to keep himself to himself."

In all his life (and this is recounted often and with puzzled awe in the lively circles he frequented) he loved only one woman, his wife, Birdeen Allen. After more than a quarter century of marriage, he was so devoted to her, so proud of her considerable beauty and so dependent on her considerable strength that he wrote her tender love sonnets. Yet even she says (as do all his friends, the intimate and the casual, men who worked hard and played hard with him, shared slit trenches and small fishing boats) that she did not entirely understand him. "I think I came closer than anybody, but I still didn't really know him. It may be that he was too complicated to be wholly known."

It may be, too, that like many writers, he revealed more of his essential self in print than he did in person. In his own opinion, the most important writing he ever did was in his five novels (*Homemade Banners, The Chartered Libertine, Peace River Country, Ask The Name of the Lion* and *The High White Forest*) and a history of Canada called *Ordeal By Fire*. He made his living, though, not as a novelist, but as a journalist. He was proud of his craft and brought to it a talent, a versatility and a drive for excellence that was unmatched by any newspaperman of his generation. In thirty-seven years, he produced well over a million words for Canadian newspapers and magazines. The articles, editorials and columns reprinted here comprise less than a twentieth of that output.

They were chosen, first of all, as I think Ralph would have wanted them to be, on the basis of their excellence and durability; some were recommended to me by old friends in the trade who had remembered a particular story or even a particular sentence for as long as twenty-five years. But despite all earnest attempts to be objective, there is no doubt that personal bias was involved in their choice and I should perhaps make clear how I knew Ralph Allen and what he meant to me.

When I met him first in the summer of 1952, he was thirty-eight years old and had been for two years the editor of *Maclean's,* a bi-weekly periodical that called itself, as it still does, Canada's national magazine.

Maclean's was then in the early years of what was to be remembered as the golden decade of Ralph Allen's editorship. In its cramped editorial offices on the fourth floor of the old cream-coloured Maclean-Hunter Publishing Company building that fronted on University Avenue at the corner of Dundas Street in downtown Toronto in those days, there was the kind of excitement that must have existed in the offices of H. L. Mencken's *American Mercury* in the Twenties or Harold Ross's *New Yorker* in the early Thirties. It was the excitement of a group of creative people who were embarked on an adventure, in the grip of what seemed to them an admirable idea.

The idea was Ralph Allen's and it was to inspire Canadian writers, artists and photographers for the next ten years and, in a way, it inspires them still. What Ralph Allen visualized, to put it simply, was a first-class magazine produced by Canadians for Canadians but without any of the diffidence or self-consciousness with which Canadian enterprises had so long been cursed. He wanted, as he said much later to the writer June Callwood, to put out a magazine that would be "both respected and read," that would give Canadians a mirror through which to view themselves and a window to view the world; that would develop standards and set tastes that would challenge a generation of Canadian journalists and engender in them a dislike for hypocrisy and a desire for excellence; that would urge its readers to look at Canada with the questioning eyes of the truly mature and at the world with the compassionate eyes of the greatly favoured. It was to be, although nobody – least of all the editor – ever said this, a magazine that reflected the aspirations and attitudes of Ralph Allen.

I knew none of this when I stepped out of the creaking cage of the single old-fashioned elevator that served the University Avenue side of the Maclean-Hunter building in those days and into the editorial offices of *Maclean's* at 8:30 on the hot morning of the first of July, 1952. In fact, I knew very little about anything. I was seventeen years old, just graduated from high school, waiting to begin university, still locked in the awful shyness of adolescence, and never to be the same again.

What ostensibly happened to me that morning was that I began a summer job as an editorial secretary (typist, copy-runner, manuscript-opener, coffee-maker) that would pay me forty dollars a week for the next ten weeks so I could earn my first-year tuition at the University of Toronto. What really happened was that I fell in love – with magazines in general, and with *Maclean's* in particular. With the smell of glue and the sight of page proofs, with the layouts on the art-department wall, with the cover paintings hung in offices and the schedule sheets clipped to beaver-boards. But most of all with the kind of people who were running that magazine, with the ideas they projected and with the *élan* with which they lived.

"To hell with Tyrone Power and boys in thick shoulder-pads and football sweaters," I said to myself at some point on that first long day. These were Writers, glamorous men of wit and grace who went out and got stories and came in and wrote well, who wore outrageously casual clothes, told outrageously boastful anecdotes and displayed outrageously iconoclastic attitudes towards established values.

When I look back now with the staler eyes of thirty-two, I realize that they cannot possibly have been as fabulous as I thought them then; that they were, in fact, an odd and untidy crew. But I do not suppose that I will ever regard with anything but affectionate respect the people who worked for Ralph Allen in those days; that I will ever again think of anyone as having as exciting and as germinal a journalistic mind as Pierre Berton displayed; or as much personal grace as Blair Fraser possessed; or as much professional know-how as Leslie Hannon, the copy editor, and Gene Aliman, the art director; or as much daring as Sidney Katz who talked to criminals and call girls, and swallowed LSD, a drug nobody had ever heard of, all in the name of *Maclean's;* or as much glamour as Barbara Moon who wrote all night and was said to own a Balenciaga; or as much caustic civility as McKenzie Porter who knew about wines and wore suède shoes in an era when Canadians drank in beer parlors and were addicted to Sunday suits.

I would like sometime to get together in a room all these people – and all the others who worked on *Maclean's* briefly or constantly during Ralph Allen's editorship: Gerry Anglin, Fred Bodsworth, N.O. Bonisteel, Carol Chapman, John Clare, Bob Collins, Barbara Dobbie, Joan Doty, Des English, Trent Frayne, Ray Gardner, John Gray, Peter Gzowski, Lois Harrison, Prue Hemelrijk, Eric Hutton, Ken Johnstone, Ken Lefolii, Carol Lindsay, David MacDonald, Shirley Mair, Herb Manning, Anne McCordick, W.O. Mitchell, Peter Newman, Jack Olsen, Ian Sclanders, Janice Tyrwhitt, Joan Weatherseed, Eva-Lis Wuorio,

Scott Young – and say to them, "Look, dammit, you weren't ordinary, were you?" I suspect most of them would answer "No, we weren't."

I think they might also be willing to attribute a good part of their feeling of self-pride to the confidence in them that Ralph Allen displayed. For at the centre of the excitement that charged the *Maclean's* offices in those days sat the editor – a tough, quick-tempered, puritanical, wise, uncompromising figure, presiding over an office full of manic-neurotic-earthy-clever people and getting out of them quality they did not know they had. It was not that he consciously set out to inspire people (he would have scoffed at the very idea), or that he treated his employees tenderly (his rages were as memorable as his praise), but that he demanded the best from the men and women he hired and the best was usually what he got.

My own first infatuation with his magazine dimmed a little during the next four winters, spent writing literary essays and arguing about God and Joe McCarthy in college common-rooms. But it bloomed again in summer vacations spent working at a variety of menial jobs in the various departments (subscription, advertising, circulation, as well as editorial) of *Maclean's* and when I went back there in the spring of 1956 as the lowliest member of the permanent editorial staff, it had changed into an ambition to become a magazine writer.

During those years *Maclean's* had grown bigger, slicker, closer to what Ralph Allen wanted it to be. It was read and heeded by everybody who mattered in this country; most of its writers, artists and cartoonists, both those on the staff and those who contributed as freelancers (Lionel Shapiro, Bruce Hutchison, June Callwood, Duncan Macpherson, George Feyer to name a few) were big names; and it was posssible for girls like me (and there were several of us with bright eyes and fresh degrees) to believe that this was the best place in the world to work.

The memories of those years, when I was a member of Ralph Allen's staff as a checker and researcher and a neophyte writer, all run together now. I can remember the autumn of Suez and the Hungarian uprising, when the office was full of excited fear, and the spring of John Diefenbaker's first triumph, when the office was full of astonishment. I can remember the smell of hops that drifted out from the nearby breweries on warm October afternoons. I can remember the dark descending on Dundas Street at four o'clock in the winter evenings, and the feeling of not wanting to go home. I can remember the whole series of agonizing stages a writer had to go through before an idea scribbled on a memo pad could be turned into a polished two-page spread in the magazine. I can remember the office parties (where the liquor consumed and the stories told were heady stuff to a girl used to cooking sherry and Presbyterian sermons) and the editorial lunches at a nearby Scandinavian restaurant on Bay Street, where ideas for future issues were put forward, embellished, shot down.

But most of all I remember Ralph Allen and trying to learn how to write first from the comments he made on established writers' manuscripts (dug out of in-baskets after five o'clock) and later from the suggestions and encouragement he and Pierre Berton, his managing editor, and Ian Sclanders, his articles editor, offered when I submitted my own beginner's efforts. I remember walking up and down the back stairs of the Maclean-Hunter building, carrying galley proofs of his editorials to the office of Floyd Chalmers, the publisher, reading as I went, and an Allen editorial on censorship was as important in my young eyes as the *Areopagitica*.

Ralph Allen was to me, then, an education, a formative influence during the formative time of my adult life. Still, it wasn't until this last winter and spring, when I re-read all of his published articles and editorials, that I fully realized how much he had formed my outlook, how many of his sensibilities and attitudes had been made my own.

I left *Maclean's* in 1959 to be married (to a *Maclean's* writer named Peter Newman), to work for another magazine, to move to another city. But Ralph and the way he thought and worked continued to be important to me; my husband was still on his staff and later, after Ralph left the editorial chair of *Maclean's* to become a contributing editor and devote more time to writing books, he came occasionally to Ottawa where we lived, and we enjoyed the benefit of his advice and the inclusive warmth of his laughter. And in 1964, when he started his fifth career as the managing editor of the *Toronto Daily Star* (with, as he wrote us, "the considered ambition of making it the best newspaper in the world") he immediately hired my husband and we had two more good years in his employ. In all that time and under all those varied circumstances, he never changed, he was never anything else to us but the best of friends and the most demanding of mentors. We continued – as we do still – to measure people newly met and admired against the tall standard set (quite unknowingly) by Ralph Allen, and to try to look at new ideas, as he said he himself tried to, in a paraphrase of one of his favourite quotations from Samuel Johnson, "with a mind cleared of cant."

The influence he had on me – and on my husband who worked for him longer and in far more important capacities – was by no means unusual, as I discovered when this book was in preparation. To his friends, his employers, his employees, to those who knew him under circumstances quite different from the ones in which I knew him, at all times and in all ways, he was special.

I hope the selections from his journalism chosen for this book will impart something of that special quality, and that they will serve to show people who did not know him, and to remind people who did, not just what manner of a writer Ralph Allen was, but what manner of a man.

Ottawa, May 1967.

CHRISTINA MCCALL NEWMAN

Ralph Allen was sixteen years old in 1930 when he climbed on a
C.P.R. train in Oxbow, Sask., with one pair of pants and something less than five dollars in his pocket, bound for Winnipeg and
a career as a newspaperman.

What the childhood he left behind was like, he never described in print and only rarely talked about, usually confining
himself to the terse details that he was born Andrew Ralph Allen
in Winnipeg on August 25, 1913, and that his family lived in a
succession of small western railroad towns before they went to
Oxbow. (Later, in his novel *Peace River Country,* he wrote that
those prairie towns with their dusty streets, false-front dry goods
stores and lonely Chinese cafés, were "much idealized by those
who have never lived there and much moved-away from by those
who have.")

He is still remembered in Oxbow as a first-rate student, an
indifferent athlete with a passionate interest in sports, and the
coronet player in the Oxbow Citizens' Band. His father, William
Glen Allen, was a C.P.R. station agent and a domineering ex-
trovert, a reader of Shakespeare and Tennyson who devoted his
spare time to writing verbose letters to editors, parliamentarians,
and kings; his mother was a quiet woman, long on common sense
and Christian principles.

The Allens had three children in addition to Ralph and very
little money. When he graduated from high school in the first dark
spring of the Depression, it was decided that they could not afford
to send him to university. Instead, William Allen wrote a letter in
praise of his son to the editor of *The Winnipeg Tribune* and armed
with that, and several clippings of hockey stories written for his
hometown paper, Ralph managed to get himself a fifteen dollar-a-
week as a reporter on the *Tribune's* sports staff.

Jim Coleman, syndicated columnist for the Southam Press,

who was also a teenaged reporter in Winnipeg in the Thirties, once described the Ralph Allen of those days as "a thin freckle-faced kid with a shock of red hair that looked like an unmade bed." He was so shy that it took the *Tribune*'s assistant sports editor, Johnny Buss, nearly six months before he realized that the "kid hanging around the office was the guy named Allen who was covering junior hockey at night and handing in his copy before I got to work."

Maurice Smith, longtime sports editor of the *Winnipeg Free Press,* then covering the same hockey beat to which Ralph was assigned, recalled that "Ralph was green in from the country and I introduced him around. But it didn't take me long to realize when I compared his copy with mine that one of us had class – and it wasn't me."

Ralph got his first break when he was sent to cover the Winnipeg hockey team at the 1932 Winter Olympics in Lake Placid, N.Y. and shortly after that, the *Tribune* gave him his own sports column. As the Thirties wore on, he wrote fewer factual reports of games and more of the kind of columns that are described in the trade as 'human interest' or 'colour' stories, but were really the response of a very sensitive and very young man to the people around him.

He was already beginning to write in the clear, balanced, *cliché*-free prose he would later perfect. According to Jim Coleman, "Before Ralph Allen, sports writing in Canada was pretty pocky stuff. He brought English to the sports pages."

He also brought a lot of laughter to the *Tribune* and anecdotes illustrating the wild Allen wit and the wilder Allen escapades were still being told in Winnipeg nearly thirty years after he had left. In his time, *Tribune* reporters were given to playing ping-pong and pop-bottle cricket in the corridors during office hours, and to shooting crap and drinking at a bootlegger's named Franny's Place after hours. Trent Frayne remembered seeing Ralph leaving Franny's with a cohort on many a morning at four A.M., just in time to meet a milk wagon at the corner of Portage and Donald. The two men would stand weaving on the sidewalk, engaged in violent argument about whose turn it was to ride the milk horse back to their boarding-house at 55 Donald. (This house is still referred to in Winnipeg – and by Winnipeggers elsewhere – as "the famous 55 Donald." Frayne, Allen, and several other reporters, including Cam MacKenzie, later of the *Saskatoon Star-Phoenix,* lived there. It was also at this address that Ralph met his future wife, Birdeen Lawrence, who had come to Winnipeg to work in 1937 after training as a nurse at the Royal Victoria Hospital in Montreal.)

Whatever game he was playing, then or later, Ralph hated to lose, always claiming that he had been out-lucked and not out-played, and blowing up in red-headed fury when his opponents made light of his efforts. He was never adverse, though, to laughing at himself and when he turned up at the *Tribune* one morning with a glowing black eye, before anybody could ask him what had happened he handed out printed cards reading, "None of your damn business."

Vince Leah, who was still at the *Tribune* writing sports after Ralph had died, fondly recalled walking along Portage Street one morning and seeing Ralph in the distance. Before he could speak, "Allen, who was covered with the ugly rash of impetigo, started to wave his hands like some Eastern untouchable and shout in a quavering sing-song 'Unclean! Keep away! Unclean!', to the considerable astonishment of the passers-by."

One night, Ralph and Cam MacKenzie, who was on the *Free Press,* came back to their rooms after spending several hours covering a game in an unheated hockey rink and drinking out of hip flasks to ward off the cold. Both had stories to file, neither felt very clear-headed. By experimenting, they discovered that MacKenzie could still move his fingers and Allen could still talk, so he dictated *two* stories (one for the *Tribune* and one for the *Free Press*) while MacKenzie typed them on copy sheets. "Even loaded, he always could write better than anybody else," is what they say in Winnipeg.

"But for all the crazy stories told about him, he was always different from the other boys," Sydney Halter, a Winnipeg lawyer and sports official, said afterwards. "There was a streak of seriousness in him that even casual friends like me could see. He read a great deal and you could tell from his copy that he was special almost from the beginning. I always said he should go to New York or somewhere in the east to work; I figured he could have been another Damon Runyon."

Ralph did go east to Toronto in December, 1938, when *The Globe and Mail* offered him a job; and the columns he wrote for the paper before he went to war are remembered still as ranking with the best of Canadian sports writing.

Reprinted here are two columns from that period on the *Globe* sports staff, one of them written the day after he arrived in

Toronto and the other written the day before he left the *Globe* to join the army. Included also are a column from the Toronto *Telegram*, from the period in 1949 when he returned briefly to writing sports, and two pieces written much later when he was managing editor of the *Toronto Daily Star,* which capture the feeling he had for sports during his early days as a reporter.

SPORTS SCRIBE INSULTED

(The Globe and Mail, December 12, 1938)

Sometime Saturday night thieves entered the hotel room occupied by Ralph Allen, of The Globe and Mail's *sports-writing staff, and stole his wallet and checks to his trunk. The trunk was recovered later, minus various items of clothing. Mr. Allen had just arrived in Toronto from Winnipeg, where he had been a sports writer on the* Tribune.

This migration business is a great thing, expecially if you are fortunate enough to own a watch-dog. Nine years ago, when I moved from Oxbow, Saskatchewan, to Winnipeg, someone stole my B-flat trumpet. Yesterday, when I moved officially from Winnipeg to Toronto, someone stole all the worldly goods I had managed to salvage from the fearful carnage of the football game in which the Argonauts took our brave Blue Bombers in the full sprightly tradition of Grant at Richmond.

I take this more as a social affront than as a mortal financial blow, for I would never seek to persuade so sophisticated a city as Toronto that sports writers can surpass that modest affluence which deems two extra suits of clothes, a spring overcoat and five dollars and two cents in cash the ultimate in lordly splendour. What annoys me most of all about the man who climbed through the transom in my hotel room Saturday night and denuded me of wallet and my slick new travelling kit and later exchanged a baggage check in the wallet for temporary custodianship of my trunk, is not his impetuous taking of liberties with a total stranger. No, there was something rather open and friendly about that. I liked the hospitable little touch when he paid the eighty-five cents storage on the trunk without a murmur and then took it out to the bank of the Humber River and left it there where Edward Stanton of 51 Brookfield Road could find it for me.

That was nice, but from there on I do not care so very much for this anonymous greeter. Why didn't he take my coon coat? That was a mighty fine coat, smart guy; my grandfather was considered a pretty nifty judge of sartorial effects. He thought so, too, when he picked it up at Isidore Fishkin Honest Loan and Used Apparel Co., Inc., on Michigan Avenue, Detroit, back in 1903. To repeat, this coon coat had something. I had visions of unveiling it to a breathless Toronto public some night in the near future and blushing at its just acclaim; long nights since I knew I was coming to work for *The Globe and Mail,* I have dreamed of sauntering easily into the press box at Maple Leaf Gardens, parading its prehensile glory while the ushers whispered to distinguished visitors, "That's that new sports writer at the *Globe,* Allen. Snappy dresser, what? They say he makes two hundred bucks a week."

What am I going to do about this coon coat now? How can this brutal disillusionment fail to slash a permanent scar across the Honest Pride Department of my wretched soul? This burglar takes all the trifling little possessions which even city editors and leg men can aspire to own. But he leaves my beautiful coon coat, unwanted, on the banks of the Humber River!

Phooey to your Toronto burglars. They're a bunch of snobs. I'll bet they wear spats.

MOSTLY INCIDENTAL

(The Globe and Mail, December 12, 1941)

Recollections of a party who is about to leave one good business for another: the ghastly, disillusioning discovery, on that very first day, that newspaper reporters don't carry shiny, black notebooks at all, but just stuff wads of copy paper in their pockets. . . . the further discovery that not one desk man in fifty wears an eye shade and that city editors are practically never addressed as "Chief." . . .

The fabulous groping for sanity in the mystic land of the expense account. . . . The first expense account, presented after a five-week trip, came to a matter of $896. . . . "Young man," the gentleman in the front office said sternly, "take this back and put another $150 on it. . . ." The second swindle sheet came to sixty-five cents for a taxi from the Royal Alexandra Hotel to downtown Winnipeg. . . . "Young man," the gentleman in the front office said sternly, "you are beating your employers out of twenty cents. . . ."

The all-day hearts games in the sports department back in Winnipeg, with Ivan Michailoff, the wrestling promoter, and Billy Burke, the fight referee, as guest stars. . . . Swearing for distance, swearing for pitch, or swearing for time, Michailoff and Burke were a two-man team for the ages. . . . The society department was right next door to the sports department, and the sound effects in that corner of the building were a riotous compound of Mike's Mujik death-bellows, Burke's North End cries for vengeance and falsetto shrieks of horror from down the hall. . . . The ears of an approaching visitor were apt to be assailed by such elevating colloquies as: "HA, ZEY STICKIT POOR OLD MICHAILOFF, ZE SONAMABLANKS – well, I never – HO (Burke cutting in), EAT THAT, YOU RUSSIAN EXPLETIVE – gentlemen, gentlemen – ZO! ZE OBSENITY SONAMA-BLANKS TRY AGAIN AT MICHAILOFF – dear me, this is disgrace – CAN YOU STAND AN OBSCENITY HEART LEAD? – really, really – ZO, ZE SONAMABLANKS VILL DUCK – gentlemen, gentle – " A resolute char-woman broke up the game for all time with the help of a heavy push-broom. . . .

Meeting Jack Dempsey, your first Grade A celebrity, in a hotel room containing at least seventy-five other rubbernecks. . . . And Dempsey walking across, as you were leaving, and saying: "Well, good-bye, Mr. Allen." You knew that remembering names was Dempsey's specialty, but that didn't take the edge off. . . .

A million hockey games, more or less. . . . Some good, some bad, but none so bad that it wasn't better than no hockey game at all. . . . The first look at the great Maple Leaf team of 1932. . . . The impression, still as vivid as ever, that Harvey Jackson was the purtiest piece of hockey machinery to look at that there ever was. . . . The night Kit Massey fired a desperate shot from his own blueline with thirteen seconds to play and scored the goal that sent the Winnipeg Elmwoods on the way to a Dominion championship. . . . The afternoon the Winnipegs were on the verge of losing the Olympic championship to the United States. . . . The coach leaning over the rail and shouting frantically at large and lazy Harold Simpson: "For God's sake get moving! There's two minutes to go." . . . Simpson grunting back, "That's lots of time," and ambling down the ice to score the tying goal. . . . The night the Rangers sank the Leafs in the finals two years ago. . . . The night the Leafs walloped Boston seven to two, last spring. . . . They were as hot that evening as hockey teams can get. . . . The personal duel between Billy Taylor and Wally Stanowski in the Oshawa-St. Boniface series. . . .

Old Satch Paige, the great Negro pitcher, turning a baseball into a small white pea, and blowing it up past the batters like a rifle bullet. . . . Red Storey submerging the beloved Bombers in the football final of 1938. . . . And, yep, Fritzie Hanson taking charge at Hamilton in 1935. . . . The conviction, though better qualified critics scream themselves black in the face, that the 1935 Bombers were the greatest Canadian football team of this generation. . . .

A little, scraggly horse called Joey, spotting bigger and nominally better horses up to twenty pounds and up to twenty lengths and running 'em down, day after day, to win by a neck at the wire. . . . Archworth hiding on the King's Plate field while the gentleman for whom the race was named stood in his box and gaped in honest admiration even as you and I. . . . Bunty Lawless and Mona Bell, and Ten to Ace, maybe the best of them all. . . .

England at Coronation time, a fine green land rejoicing in the deathless things that made it fine. . . . The Palace, the Abbey, St. Paul's, the Strand, the Mall, Hyde Park, all of them exactly the way they should have been, and the way they must be again. . . . A sunny little village forty miles down the Seine from Paris. . . .

The people you have worked for and with. . . . Never having owned a newspaper or even exercised authority over any one in the business except an occasional timid office boy, we are in no position to say what makes a good employer and what doesn't. . . . But if we are ever required to make any research on the subject of human, sympathetic and generous bosses, we'll be able to fill the slate, from the top down, without going off these premises. . . .

In another minute we'll be showing you our appendix scars. . . . All we wanted to let you know in the first place was that

"Mostly Incidental" is herewith trading one newspaper "thirty" for one regimental number, and that we're sorry to say good-bye.

WANTED: SIX GO-GETTING MIDGETS

(The Toronto Telegram, March 7, 1949)

Wanted: Six to twelve go-getting, clean-living midgets to work in sports department of established metropolitan newspaper. Maximum height 3 feet six inches, maximum weight 35 pounds. Knowledge of English grammar, hockey, baseball and football an asset but not essential. Here is a real opportunity for the midget of vision and ambition to enter a career with a genuine future. Interested midgets should apply, giving waist, chest and calf measurements, to Personnel Dept., *The Evening Telegram,* Bay Street, Toronto.

There has been a great deal of talk around town, some of it true, about the streamlining of this journal, but in one respect it is still the same old *Telegram,* only more so. Always notorious for its cosiness and intimacy, even in the days when Mr. Fitz was putting out the pages with the help of one rather undernourished cub, the physical habitat of the sports department still retains the pristine dimensions conferred on it by the late John Ross Robertson. These, by actual measurement, are: length twenty-two feet; width eighteen feet. The normal population of same, by actual count, now consists of eleven adult males, not counting such floaters as publicity men, office boys, bill collectors, fight promoters, angry wives, inventors of new systems for making racetrack selections, insurance salesmen, meddlesome employers, printers and other traditional links between the sports writer and civilization at large.

In addition to these human occupants, the enlarged telephone booth into which they are fitted contains the following major items of furniture and literature: ten large-sized desks, ten large-sized chairs, one large wastepaper basket, three small wastepaper baskets, ten glue pots, three coat racks, one medium-sized ashtray, three old overshoes, four wall calendars, two record books, one hundred and thirteen empty Coca-Cola bottles and two copies of last night's pink edition.

You might think this is impossible, and you would almost be right. Actually, if everybody who is supposed to work here showed up at one time, it would take a hydraulic press to squeeze us all in, even in theory. Mr. Robert Hewitson, who is in charge of the seating arrangements, has worked out a complicated diagram purporting to show that if all eleven of the nominal residents appeared at once, we could just make it by having a masseur come in to have a fast, last-minute go at Bunny Morganson, jettisoning our coats and vests out the window and inducing the last man through the door to lie down on the floor.

Despite Hewitson's show of confidence, I believe he is living in a fool's paradise. Already I see signs of a crack in his nerve. The week-end before last he sent a writer named Reeve to Florida. Last week-end he sent a writer named Frayne to Florida. God knows whose turn will be next. Every now and then I see him glancing my way, his eyes glinting speculatively like the man in charge of a lifeboat with the water running low. Just let him try that Florida ruse on me and see how far he gets. They promised me a chair and a desk all to myself when I came here, see, Hewitson, and I don't care if you offer to fly me to Tahiti in a sarong, I'm standing on my rights.

So far Hewitson has had a pretty good run of luck. One day a couple of weeks ago, before he started driving his loyal colleagues off to Miami, we actually had nine sports writers in here all at once and it looked pretty dark. Just then the phone rang. Hewitson got to it by crawling on his hands and knees and chasing a couple of intervening authors under their desks with a copy spike. He listened for a minute and then a radiant smile broke over his face.

"Johnny Fitzgerald is sick," he said.

When Hewitson extricated his foot from my mouth, I spat out a couple of teeth and mumbled a few words of anxious inquiry.

"Heart!" Hewitson said happily.

Three days after that, Hewitson announced that another of the field hands, Bob Hesketh, was sick too.

"Medical science is baffled," Hewitson said, rubbing his hands. "It may be weeks before they even get the case diagnosed."

"Poor old Hesketh," one of his fellow swinkers sighed. "I'll borrow his desk."

"One of Nature's noblemen," another colleague murmured while the tears streamed down his face. "As long as he won't be needing it I might as well carve my initials on that chair."

17

So for the time being, the pressure is off. Just the same, I shudder to think where we'll be if our comfy little group ever runs out of winter resorts or diseases. I still think the far-sighted, permanent solution would be to import a plane-load of pygmies and teach them to spell.

CANADA'S GAME RETURNS TO GLORY

(The Toronto Star, May 3, 1965)

For twenty-seven glorious minutes last Saturday night Canada came close to rediscovering the only unique part of its inheritance. In spite of what they'll say in the commissions on culture and the proliferating expositions and festivals and aids-in-grant to anybody who knows anybody else, the only true Canadian invention is a game called hockey.

And hockey, this most priceless ingredient of the Canadian tradition had been, until those first magic twenty-seven minutes of a magic hockey game on Saturday, a ruin and a mockery.

They had changed it from a tough but lovely form of art into a double-barrelled exercise in delinquency – the juveniles on the ice, the adults in the eight-dollar seats up above. The grace and dash and style were gone – all gone in a hideous swamp of haul and tug and grab and kick and poke and punch and howl and shout and screech and jeer, sticks in the teeth, knees in the groin, skates in the ankle, kill the referee.

But for twenty-seven minutes in the Montreal Forum on Saturday night they went back to playing hockey and for anyone lucky enough to be there – not watching in the greys of television but really there in the Forum – it was an unforgettable experience. The Canadiens went on the ice with a young and eager team led by an old and eager man named Jean Beliveau. They were as fresh and fiery and exciting to watch as a well-trained platoon of infantry fighters.

They passed the puck with crazy confidence and crazier precision, throwing it at sixty miles an hour half the length of the ice, stick-blade to stick-blade, neither man missing half a step. Their checking was superb, particularly on the defence, and it wasn't the grab-and-fall-down or slug-and-holler checking they've sold so hard and successfully on Eighth Avenue in New York and Carlton Street in Toronto.

It was stick-checking, playing the puck or, if playing the man, trying to steer or outmanoeuvre him rather than to elbow, knee or board him.

It was hockey they were playing for that period and a third in Montreal – hockey such as this generation hardly knows about or even suspects.

Just the same I won't go back. This brief display of hockey was only an anachronism, an accident, a fault in the main structure.

I had felt I would never go to another hockey game as long as I lived until a persuasive and kindly friend of mine cornered me in Montreal and said he had the two best seats in the house and I must come with him.

I said I appreciated the invitation but indicated without much subtlety that I would have preferred an invitation to a hanging.

"You're just being modest," my friend said. "Everybody wants to go to this hockey game. This is the seventh and final game. I've got you in."

I notified him, vainly, that the Galerie Martal even at that instant was displaying a wide selection of works by artists of L'Ecole de Paris. I felt it fair to add that the horses were going at Blue Bonnets, Van Cliburn was about to play the piano at the Place des Arts, and according to the usually reliable *Montreal Star* there were Girls Girls Girls at the Montrose, Jazz Jazz Jazz at the Black Bottom and all the lobsters you could eat for five dollars at the Grand Motor Hotel, 6126 Cote de Liesse Road.

He would not be swayed. The hour drew nearer. I reminded him that two of our mutual friends, Conn Smythe and Clarence Campbell, were responsible for sanctifying the elbow as the most important instrument in hockey and said it would be a shame to go and witness their continued disgrace.

"Don't worry," he said. "Best seats in the house."

I got him to Mother Martin's. We had double scotches.

"Time to go," he said. "The traffic around the Forum gets tough on hockey nights."

I reminded him of other matters. That they quit making hockey players when they were through with Busher Jackson and just conceivably Milt Schmidt. He said Bill Cook was pretty good and I accepted that. We could find no agreement on Eddie Shore, greatly overrated in my opinion. There was a little desultory talk about Syl Apps but as my friend pointed out Apps kept racing into the corners and so we were forced to dismiss him from the conversation.

We had *escargots bourguignons*. They do them very well at Mother Martin's.

"If we get a cab right now. . . ." my friend said.

I pointed out that Rocket Richard and Gordie Howe, while both loaded with talent, had finally been forced to compete with the grabbers and haulers. Bobby Hull, the only other first-rate player of this generation, has been driven into the same predicament by the weird philosophy imposed on the game by Smythe and Campbell.

We got to the game anyway. There was no helping it. My friend is a very stubborn man.

As we sat down, somebody was blowing a trumpet and fourteen thousand presumably sane people were already shrieking wild maledictions at everybody in sight.

I turned and beamed at the harridan right behind us.

"My friend," I said, "is one of the owners of the Chicago team." (Actually he is from Winnipeg.)

Every time Montreal scored she hit him on the head with her umbrella and shouted some new insult at him. It would have been a good game even if she hadn't.

BOXING STILL HAS ROOM FOR HONEST MEN

(The Toronto Star, May 29, 1965)

Unlike some of the people who watched the seedy demise of Sonny Liston the other night and the equally seedy triumph of Cassius Clay, I left the arena with mixed thoughts. I did not share the general view that boxing never would be and never had been for anybody but bums.

Boxing has occasionally – though only occasionally – been good and honest to the men who have been good and honest to it.

I went out of the grievous Clay-Liston farce thinking of my old friend, Jimmy McLarnin.

Jimmy McLarnin, without question, was one of the greatest boxers since the dawn of the Marquis of Queensberry. He came off a newsboy's beat on a wharf in Vancouver almost forty-five years ago, hungry, twelve years old and eager, and he met an old booth fighter from England named Charlie Foster, nicknamed Pop. Four years later, when McLarnin was sixteen, he and Pop Foster left Vancouver, still broke and unknown.

In the next thirteen years, with Foster acting as his teacher, manager and best friend, McLarnin fought and beat a total of thirteen world champions – reigning, past or to-be. He became a world champion himself and in 1950 was elected to boxing's Hall of Fame to join a circle of only fourteen men with names like John L. Sullivan, James J. Corbett, Bob Fitzsimmons, James J. Jeffries, Jack Dempsey and Joe Louis.

Jimmy was up here a couple of weeks ago to appear on one of those mystery-guest shows on CBC Television. We had a long, nostalgic lunch together and although Jimmy doesn't talk much about his fights any more, we talked a while about fighting.

With the ancient courtesy that old prize-fighters so often show toward new ones he said Liston wasn't bad, although a little slow; he said Clay was fairly good; he said Patterson was pretty good; he said George Chuvalo, his fellow Canadian, was promising. This of course was all arrant nonsense and we both knew it. Jimmy never weighed more than one hundred and fifty-seven pounds in his life and he personally could have beaten all these alleged heavy-weights in one night, one at a time or all together.

What got me reflecting, though, were things McLarnin had said on other things. He's now a millionaire, or close to it, and close to retiring in a comfortable suburb of Los Angeles, but he's never been able to forget the little boy from Vancouver.

I couldn't help contrasting Jimmy's eager honesty, in many talks in times past, with the sullen, bovine, cynical indifference of Liston and the lunatic braggadocio of Clay.

This is what Jimmy McLarnin said to me once and I took it down and it is exact: "When I was fighting I gave the job everything I had. I trained hard and fought hard. After my winning fights I'd turn a handspring in the ring and Pop Foster would wrap me in an emerald dressing-gown decorated with a golden harp. Then I'd head up the aisle behind a bunch of Irish cops and if the fight had happened to be a real good one those wonderfully emotional Irish fans who used to come to my fights would break through the cops and carry me to the dressing-room on their shoulders."

A little later Jimmy said: "It's not fair to expect anyone who hasn't been through it himself to understand what you have to do to succeed as a professional boxer. Boxing was my business from

21

the time I was 12. I had nothing to start with except a quick, wiry pair of legs and Pop's promise that he would make me a champion of the world if I did what he told me to."

I got Jimmy talking about some of his fights again and I kept trying to tell him this was a racket fight coming up, a dive.

He wouldn't make a guess himself. But after the Clay-Liston fight was over I went back and looked up something Jimmy McLarnin had written with my help 15 years ago. This is it:

I was never asked to throw a fight or offered a bribe, a threat or any other kind of inducement to throw a fight. Neither was Pop.

We were told twice by managers of other fighters that their fighters couldn't fight me unless I'd agree not to try to knock them out. Once, in our early days in Oakland before Pop and I had a written contract and all we had to eat was the crabs we could net in San Francisco Bay, one of those strangely prosperous little men who hang around gyms told me that if I'd get rid of Pop he'd see that I got all the steaks and all the fights I could handle.

Another time, after things were going better for us, a "New York manager" wrote and urged me to quit wasting my time in the tall timber and come and get it where the getting was good. Of course, he added, I would have to place myself in the hands of somebody who knew the right people and had the necessary ins – meaning him.

None of these propositions got as far as the discussion stage. To the best of my knowledge they were the only propositions of a dishonest or doubtful nature that were ever put to either Pop or me.

This wasn't entirely an accident. It was Pop's theory that nobody ever made a proposition without first finding somebody to listen to it – and Pop was a terrible listener. Even when we were going our biggest in New York, we spent as little time there as possible. We usually trained at Gus Wilson's camp at Orangeburg, New York, or Madame Biers' camp at Pompton Lakes, New Jersey, and came into town the afternoon before the fight. We made a practice of staying in the wrong hotels – small, chintzy places populated largely by old ladies and Pomeranians. The night before the fight we'd usually go to a late show, partly to get my mind off the fight and partly to help me sleep a little later than usual the next morning.

The morning after the fight we'd go downtown and pick up our cheque from Tex Rickard or Mike Jacobs or whoever the promoter was and then we'd drive to Long Island, where we had a house and some property for a few years. More often we'd fly out to Los Angeles and either stay there until it was time to come back east and start training for the next fight, or go on up to Vancouver.

So we weren't too accessible to strangers – especially suspicious strangers – and all strangers were suspicious to Pop. I was far more guileless than he was, but I only got close once to striking up a genuine acquaintance with a real live gangster. The day after one of my fights I went downtown with my brother Bob, who had been helping me with my training. We weren't leaving town until late at night and before I left I wanted a piece of lemon pie. In or out of training I was always very careful about my diet. According to my theories and Pop's on food, pastry of any kind has all the health-giving properties of arsenic. But I've got a hopeless weakness for lemon pie and after an earlier fight I'd discovered a restaurant that made the best lemon pie in the world.

Bob and I were sitting alone eating our lemon pie when the owner of the restaurant came up and said he'd like to introduce us to some men sitting at another table. We took our pie over and sat down for a while with Legs Diamond and his bodyguard. Prohibition was still in force and Diamond, who was murdered about a year later, was then undisputed king of rackets. Bob and I sat around chatting with Diamond and his boys for half an hour or so, mostly about fights and fighters and then we said good-by and went home.

I told Pop where we'd been and what we'd had to eat. He frowned a little when I mentioned the lemon pie but didn't say anything. Then I told him who we'd been talking to.

I never heard Pop use a swear word until I was past thirty. This time it looked close. He didn't say anything for almost a minute. When he finally spoke his voice was under perfect control.

"Jimmy," he said. "Don't ever eat lemon pie with Legs Diamond again."

"Okay, Pop," I said.

"And Jimmy."

"Yes, Pop?"

"Don't even eat a nice healthy salad with Legs Diamond."

"I won't, Pop," I said, and I never did.

Those were Jimmy McLarnin's recollections of a long time ago.

Whatever else they prove or fail to prove, they offer some evidence that even the soiled and sordid sport of boxing once had room for decent men.

Who knows? Perhaps it still has.

PART II WAR

On December 8, 1941, the day after Pearl Harbor, Ralph Allen joined the army as a gunner in the Royal Canadian Artillery. He went overseas the next year as a gun-crew sergeant with the 30th Anti-Aircraft Battery – called the "sportsmen's brigade" and commanded by Major Conn Smythe of the Maple Leaf hockey team.

While he was an N.C.O., Ralph contributed to the *Globe* a series of humorous columns on army life that ran under the title "The Sarge", and early in 1943 he was discharged, on the *Globe*'s initiative, to become that paper's war correspondent.

Until then, except for six months in 1937 when he went to Europe with Frank Emma, a friend from Winnipeg, and sent back to the *Tribune* occasional feature stories about his trip, and a short period at the *Globe* when he did general reporting, he had spent all his working life covering sports.

In the next thirty months, he turned himself into a journalist of the first rank, filing hundreds of front-line reports that were considered at the time by civilians, soldiers and other correspondents to be outstanding. After nearly a quarter of a century, these reports are still undimmed in their perception and unsettling in their poignancy; as evocative to the non-participant of the horror and glory of that war as any novel or history of the period.

He made the first-day landings with the Canadian troops in Italy and the D-Day landing in France; he saw all the major battles of the war in which the Canadian army was involved; he was there when Paris was liberated, when the Rhine was crossed and when the first war criminals were tried at Nuremberg. He was

25

noted for keeping close to the action and close to the common soldier. He had an awesome disdain for what he called the "brass" and a particular dislike for army P.R. men whom he suspected of wanting to keep all those seeking to be "Boswell to the belligerents . . . in the warlike atmosphere of a press room, miles behind the front . . . digesting handouts, arguing with censors and generally leading the heady and dangerous existence of a neurotic scoutmaster."

Among his fellow correspondents (a group that included Gregory Clark, Jam Cook, Fred Griffin, Matthew Halton, Charles Lynch, Ross Munro, Lionel Shapiro, Wallace Reyburn, Peter Stursberg and Sholto Watt), who were for the most part a brave and talented lot, he was much admired for his bravery and his talent. It was the carbon copies of Allen's stories that most of them wanted to read at the end of the day, although he was far more reticent about handing them around than Halton, who was the CBC's man at war and was given to reading aloud his radio scripts in a plummy voice, or Shapiro, one of Ralph's greatest friends then and later, who would pull his last sheet of copy from his typewriter, mount a table, wave the press room to silence and then announce in a clear voice, "I have written a magnificent story, a positively magnificent story."

Ross Munro, a gentle and perceptive journalist who, as the Canadian Press war correspondent, was four years on the battlefronts, and later became publisher of *The Winnipeg Tribune* and *The Canadian* magazine, spent the night of the sixth of June, 1944, in a slit trench in a French orchard on the front line, with Ralph Allen as his companion.

"He didn't show any particular emotion of fear, that night or ever, but he didn't make any phony attempts at stoicism either," Munro remembered afterwards. "He was always the most human of beings; modest about his own accomplishments, sometimes irritable, often funny. He wasn't strong – when I saw him first in England he was still with Conn Smythe's brigade and I remember wondering how he'd got into the army – he was sick several times with infections, but he'd drive himself hard, riding all day in a jeep and writing by flashlight, growling with contempt if you offered him sympathy. He pretended to be tough but the terrible things we saw had a deep effect."

He wrote pessimistic letters home to his managing editor, R.A. Farquharson of the *Globe,* complaining testily about the way his copy was handled and predicting gloomily that war and destruction would never end. This gloom was rarely reflected in his writing and certainly never showed in his dress.

As Trent Frayne wrote in *Liberty* magazine at the time, Ralph had a reputation for being "next to General Montgomery, the most unusual dresser in the entire Allied forces." His "uniform" consisted of "a pair of yellow corduroy breeches . . . a stretched and faded turtle-neck sweater, covered by a rumpled battle dress blouse . . . a beret . . . and scuffed Oxfords instead of boots."

In the fall of 1944, when an investiture ceremony was scheduled in Belgium, an order came through that Canadian correspondents were to appear in dress uniform because the Belgian King was to officiate. "Allen did pretty well," according to Ross Munro. "He wore a fine new officer's hat, his greatcoat was pressed, and his shoes were highly polished. But between the tops of his shoes and the bottom of his greatcoat there emerged those ghastly yellow corduroys. We relegated him to the back row of our line-up, and there he stood during the ceremony, muttering darkly about narrow-minded war correspondents and accusing the 'brass' of interfering with the freedom of the press."

On another occasion Allen was caught, "in a rain of mortars from a German weapon known as the Moaning Minnie," said Charles Lynch who was with him. "We took refuge behind a stone wall. As the stuff kept coming down, Allen finally stuck his foot out from behind the wall and shouted: 'All right, you bastards, take that leg and leave me the rest.' "

Ralph rarely wrote about his own exploits, used the pronoun "I" sparingly in his copy and generally presented himself as a Schweik-like bumbler.

From his accounts of the war that follow here, it should be evident that he was anything but bumbling – rather that he was courageous, eloquent and, more important, just; that he could look with as much sympathy on German refugees as he did on the plight of French children.

"For me," Ross Munro said later, "his particular brand of fairness was never more evident than at the Nuremberg trials in the fall of 1945. When most of us were leaning hard on restitution and patriotism, Ralph was trying to place the miseries of that particular war, suffered by our enemies and our allies, in the broad picture of human suffering."

London (April 14, 1943)

During sixteen months as a private soldier and N.C.O. in the Canadian Army, this retired warrior conducted himself with such wary piety that the conduct sheet of B-18789, Sgt. Allen, A.R., ended with the rare and saintly footnote: "Entries nil." No crimes. No charges. Not even an admonishment or a reprimand.

And then the Army discharged me to become a war correspondent. And within twelve hours of my release from the vast hair-trigger orbit of military law I was arrested by the Canadian Provost Corps, whisked in an Army Black Maria to a four-story guardhouse in the heart of London, and charged with enough crimes to drive a general court-martial to drink.

The fault belongs to (a) London's crowded housing conditions and (b) me. After receiving my discharge certificate at a transit depot in Surrey, I took a train to London, arriving late in the evening – much too late, as it turned out, to find a hotel. Being officially a civilian, I was not eligible for lodging in any of the service hostels. After several hours of vain and weary searching, I wandered into a Y.M.C.A. canteen on the Strand some time after midnight, scored an unoccupied easy chair and fell into the sleep of the just but homeless.

I was wearing battle dress, from which I had removed my sergeant's stripes, battle patches and Canada and RCA badges. By replacing them with special badges, I could transform my battle dress into the authorized uniform of a Canadian war correspondent.

I can see now that, from the provost corporal's point of view, snoring there blissfully at three o'clock in the morning in a uniform divested of official insignia – and, moreover, wearing a collar and tie which is *verboten* to private soldiers – I must have looked like one of military society's most sinister enemies.

The corporal prodded me gently but enthusiastically. My subconscious interpreted the gesture as part of the dream I was having.

"Quit pushing," I mumbled to my Vice-President in charge of Dreams, and settled deeper in the chair.

"Where's your pass?"

"No pass," I grunted testily, and made a mental note to tell the Vice-President in charge of Dreams that, effective immediately, we were free to stop dreaming about the small annoyances of military life, anyway.

"Then you're on the loose." This was accompanied by a shake that, although polite enough, could not possibly be confused with the gossamer stuff of dreams.

I opened one eye and got my first look at the corporal.

"Who are you?" the corporal said.

"I'm a civilian," I said.

"You look like a soldier to me," the corporal said. "You're in a soldier's canteen, you're wearing a soldier's uniform, you haven't got a pass and you're improperly dressed."

"All right, I'm a soldier," I said desperately. "But if I'm a soldier I'm a sergeant, and you'll have to get a sergeant to take me in."

"Well, well," the corporal said. "You learn something every day. I used to think sergeants wore stripes. Would you mind just sitting right there while I call the wagon?"

At the guardroom, the corporal told his story briefly, succinctly and with occasional traces of emotion.

"This guy," the corporal sobbed to his sergeant, "has all the outward appearances of a private soldier. He says he's a civilian. A war correspondent. Then he says he's a sergeant. He hasn't got a pass and he says he isn't on the loose."

"All right," the sergeant said affably, "which is it?"

At this point I suddenly remembered that war correspondents attached to the Canadian Army hold the honorary rank of captain.

"I guess," I said, "that for military purposes I am a captain."

The corporal slowly began to beat his head with his fists. The sergeant tried to look patient.

"Migawd, another promotion?" he gulped. "You've certainly had a spectacular career."

"Well," I said modestly, "I'm not really a captain. Just an honorary captain."

"Honorary captain now," the corporal sighed. "The only honorary captains I know about are chaplains."

"Recite the beatitudes!" the sergeant snapped craftily.

I admitted sadly that I couldn't.

"Whatever this bird is," the corporal said, "he's already impersonated more people than Gracie Fields."

"Take him upstairs," the sergeant commanded.

Upstairs the senior sergeant spent ten minutes examining my papers and finally let me go. I returned gratefully to the blackout and the blitz.

EASTER BELLS

London (By mail, printed May 17, 1943)

Being an unretouched, chronological account of a Canadian reporter's attempt to get a story on the ringing of the bells at Westminster Abbey on Easter Sunday:

Easter Saturday, 1:32 P.M.: reporter, fumbling through pockets for identity card, discovers scribbled memo to self reading as follows: "Government ban on ringing of church bells, except for invasion, ends on Easter Sunday. Go to Abbey. Interview bellringers. Interview elderly clerics. Get elderly clerics' refreshing reactions."

Easter Saturday, 1:50 P.M.: reporter enters Abbey, experiencing same thrill as always on entering sacred shrine of Empire. Asks guide who would be likeliest party to interview on subject of bells. Is referred to Rev. Dr. – , whom investigation discloses to be a high official of the Abbey, with nine letters after his name.

1:55 P.M.: reporter finds Rev. Dr. – in choir boys' room. In long black robes, white-haired, kindly Dr. – makes perfect picture of senior ecclesiastic.

1:56 P.M.: Dr. – obligingly steps into adjoining cloister. Acknowledges reporter's introduction. Cut to conversation:

DR. – : Well, well, my boy, so you're a journalist.

REPORTER: Yes, sir. I wanted to do a story on the ringing of the bells tomorrow. I thought it must mean a lot to you people who live here in the Abbey. I know it will mean a lot to thousands of people back in my country who have never even seen the Abbey.

DR. – : Um. (Reporter makes mental note reminding self to include paragraph about eager glow which suffused elderly cleric's face at mention of beloved chimes.)

DR. – : Well, you have come to the right source for your story. I know more than any man living about the bells of the Abbey. I have made a lifelong study of them.

REPORTER: This is very gratifying.

DR. – : So if your paper wants me to do a story on the bells, I should be delighted to do so. On a business basis, of course. (Reporter makes mental note reminding self to forget paragraph about eager glow suffusing elderly cleric's face. Is still convinced he saw eager glow, but now suspects he misinterpreted its meaning.)

REPORTER: I'm afraid you misunderstood me. I was going to write the story myself. I do not expect you to give me access to your expert knowledge. I merely hoped for a few general observations on the meaning of the occasion, as viewed through the eyes of a servant of the Church.

DR. – : You may quote me as saying that the bells of Westminster Abbey will ring tomorrow at 3 P.M.

REPORTER: Possibly it could be arranged for me to talk to one of the bell-ringers?

DR. – : It could be arranged through me. I am in charge of the bell-ringers. But I'm afraid none of them are around just now, and I'm sure I don't know where to look for them.

REPORTER: Suppose I come back tomorrow?

DR. – : I don't think that would do any good. It would be impossible to admit you to the belfry.

REPORTER: Well, good afternoon.

DR. – : I hope you understand my position.

REPORTER: Perfectly.

DR – : You are a business man. I am a business man. Good afternoon.

Easter Sunday, 3 P.M.: historic chimes of Westminster Abbey peal out over London, carrying a new saga of hope and inspiration to the world. Reporter sits in Leicester Square cinema, watching Joan Crawford ham up another one.

CHURCHILL IN THE COMMONS

London (By mail, June 18, 1943)

For much the same reason that no man can be a hero to his valet, it is difficult for a Prime Minister to be a hero to the English House of Commons, even when the House is virtually without an Opposition. Nevertheless, Mr. Churchill is as much a hero in the square snug chamber in Westminster as in the Lion's Head at

31

Bethnal Green, the Horse and Groom at Paisley and the Boar's Head in that quaint little town in Cornwall.

Although the benches of this eight-year-old Parliament are filled with people who knew him when, the electric thrill that runs through the Commons as he rises to address the Speaker is as unmistakeable and elemental as the light that shines in a small boy's eyes when he shakes hands with Jack Dempsey.

To a degree that can't be measured in terms of votes, Mr. Churchill is the Big Guy in the Commons, and knows it. He is far too old a Parliamentarian to patronize his Parliament, even if he ever felt the temptation. But he is also too old a Parliamentarian not to know that his personal hold on the members is an asset of the nation, and that as such it's well worth cultivating.

It may be for this reason that a speech by Churchill to the Commons usually has its special tones and touches, and that if you're lucky enough to hear one you are likely to remember it as a performance even after you have forgotten some of it as a speech.

No one ever "knows" when Mr. Churchill is going to speak these days. No one except the members even "knows" on what days the House will sit. But when it was announced immediately after the Prime Minister's return from his visit to Washington and North Africa that he would report to the House at some time during the next series of sittings, a large number of people with Whitehall, Embassy or newspaper connections were given cause to suspect that report would start sometime around noon on Tuesday, June 8.

When this writer presented himself to the reception office to exchange Pass Number One for Pass Number Three and sign the second of three registers you must endorse before being admitted to the Strangers' Gallery, an important-looking usher was saying into a telephone: "Number Ten Downing Street? Has that package left yet? Thank you." It did not seem prudent at the time to inquire into the meaning of this mysterious fragment of conversation, but until somebody explodes my lovely little myth, I'm going to go right on believing that on at least one day during the Second Great War the secret-service code-word for Winston Churchill was "package."

The Chamber of the Lords, pre-empted more than two years ago by the bombed-out Commons, filled up fast as Ministers and Under-Secretaries plodded through their daily chore of persuading the back-benchers, during questions period, that Ministers and

Under-Secretaries know what's going on in their own departments. There isn't room to fit all the 615 members into the Commons' emergency quarters, and after all the available seats had been taken up, there were still three standees left beside the Sergeant-at-arms.

The Ambassadors', Ladies', Strangers' and Members' Galleries, none of them large enough to keep a Punch-and-Judy show in business, sprouted a luxuriant crop of celebrities—Ambassadors Winant, Maisky and the Duke of Alba, Mrs. Churchill and Mrs. Eden, Field Marshal Wavell; John Steinbeck, wearing the uniform of an American war correspondent; dozens of peers.

Lord Simon, the Lord Chancellor, arrived late and had to settle for a seat on the canopy of the throne. At the furthermost peak of the canopy, right under the ceiling, Lord Brabazon peered down on the floor of the House like a lost steeplejack.

Questions were almost over when Mr. Churchill arrived through an entrance behind the Speaker's chair. At first the effect of his entrance was lost in the Strangers' Gallery, for two reasons: the first being that he was not immediately visible from there, and the second being that when an English M.P. cheers, he attempts to do so without making a noise.

My own impression, as the first members to catch sight of the Prime Minister rose to their feet waving their arms excitedly and giving voice to the muffled Parliamentary tiger, was that a fire must have broken out somewhere behind the Speaker and that the members who had noticed were anxious to call attention to it without creating too violent a disturbance. But as the Prime Minister entered the full orbit of the House's view, the inhibited growls of approval swelled to a full-scale rumble.

Mr. Churchill smiled faintly and walked quickly to a seat on the front bench between Mr. Clement Atlee, the Laborite Deputy Prime Minister, and Sir Archibald Sinclair, the Liberal Air Minister.

Ten minutes later questions were over and Mr. Churchill rose to his feet, adjusted his horn-rimmed glasses, took a couple of steps to the Speaker's table, laid his notes carefully on it and began to speak.

I'd heard most of the other senior Ministers speak at some time or other; the first and most obvious difference about Mr. Churchill was that, with the possible exceptions of Mr. Eden and Home Secretary Herbert Morrison, he is the only Minister who fully appreciated the advantage of having every word heard clearly in every corner of the House.

Practically all the Ministers trust the microphone near the front benches to pick up their speeches without troubling themselves too much about the technical aspects of the matter. Mr. Churchill checked his range to the mike several times out of the corner of an eye.

Beyond all approval for what he said and beyond all gratitude for the personal efforts that made it possible for him to say it, the speech created a mood among the members that could be described as a mood of sheer delight.

Mr. Churchill didn't say much that his followers didn't know before. He said that "amphibious operations of peculiar complexity and hazard on a large scale are approaching." He said that the U-boat was going better than it had gone since 1941. He said that our aim is the complete destruction of our foes.

It was a fine speech, but it was not so newsworthy as the speech he had made three weeks before to the United States Congress. The point is that, so complete was the bond between the man down there beside the Speaker's table and the people listening to him on the floor of the House, you were sure in the galleries that he could have described a Scottish sunset or something equally irrelevant and still have held his audience enthralled.

This wasn't merely a great warrior back from a great journey, you felt; it was a great House of Commons man showing a House of Commons what makes a Commons man great.

He warned the Commons – "We have still to show that we can keep ourselves at the height and level of successful events, and to be worthy of good fortune."

He apologized to the Commons – "I have already given to the joint sessions of the Congress of the United States the statements which I should have made to this House on the victories in Tunisia, had I been in this country."

He praised the Commons – "The foundation and instrument for the waging of a successful war and for the safety of the State were never surpassed in modern or ancient times."

He referred often to his notes, but often he left the notes and the audience both behind and went on to what amounted to private raiding parties into the vast sphere of his eloquence. At these times, the House held its breath while Mr. Churchill's expressive arms cut the air as though he were grasping physically for the word he wanted. He always got it within a second. When he sat

34

down and the peculiar semi-noiseless Commons cheering started again, it was obvious they weren't only cheering a great statesman and a great warrior. They were cheering a personal hero of theirs. Carrying the water bucket in for The Champ.

THE CAVES, THE VILLAS, THE KITCHENS OF ITALY

Reggio, Calabria – Italy (September 3, 1943)

Wanted: in or near a beach, a small residence, suitable for six transient professional men. Heat, light, water, telephone, maid service, plumbing or furniture not necessary, but quiet is essential.

From the standpoint of housing, war correspondents are sometimes the most favoured class in the world and sometimes the most underprivileged. The dull but secure monotony of a mosquito net and blankets under olive or lemon trees in a regimental bivouac area is not a problem. The panting Boswells look after their own housing in the earliest and latest stages of most campaigns.

The night before last I slept on a scented terrace in a twenty-room villa on the lower slopes of Mount Etna. Tonight – all right then, what about tonight?

In nine hours since we landed in Italy this morning, three authors, one radio technician and two conducting officers who comprise the advance headquarters of the Canadian Army's Mediterranean public relations service, have already had four more or less official places of residence.

The first was on the edge of the beach where we threw our blankets, web equipment and typewriters in the first light of dawn. Traffic beat us there. We left along a cluttered, clanking, sandy highway in response to advice from Ross Munro, Canadian Press reporter, that he had found "the ideal spot" further inland.

This ornament to the real estate industry turned out to be a series of tiny oblong caves set back of a narrow ledge along a steep cliff-face overlooking the harbour.

"Cosy and secluded," Munro beamed unctuously as we made the back-breaking climb and settled down to work. "A home and an office in one."

This undernourished grotto made a good office for a couple of hours, but deficiencies as a dormitory soon showed up. We did a little work, then stretched out one man to a cave to catch some sleep.

Suddenly a deafening crash rolled around the corner, stopped, turned back, pushed on into the caves, looked around for a while like a prospective tenant and then plunged on into the distance, leaving the whole ridge quivering like an embryonic earthquake. A high screeching whine followed.

Then the whole business was repeated and repeated again. We knew the worst. Our little nest lay right under the muzzles of the first Allied gun emplacements to be set up in that sector.

We stuck it out gamely, dozing off in snatches between salvos. Then a louder, much more insistent screech filled the shaking catacombs and plummeted down the musical scale into the deafening basso of the first enemy bomb falling less than a hundred yards away. The walls of our caves began to crumble gently, dropping a carpet of fine sand and pebbles from the roof.

We moved again.

This time we were lucky enough to find room in a ground-floor apartment in town.

Housewives from two stories above have been bringing their children down regularly for the last two hours to peer over our shoulders at our copy, giving vent to clucks of encouragement by way of introduction and then telling us about their uncles in Pittsburgh. They all have uncles in Pittsburgh, and what's more, they'll show you pictures to prove it.

How values change. Only a few weeks ago it was news when you turned up an Italian who had an uncle in Pittsburgh. If I ever find another one who hasn't an uncle in Pittsburgh I won't stop writing until the editor hollers for mercy.

The hubbub created by dozens of neighbours telling us about trans-offspring and enlivening otherwise unintelligible conversations with irrelevant cries of "bono" are beginning to make us wonder if our little caves in the cliff weren't a rest home after all.

Munro made the mistake of asking one of our neighbours for a chair. The little man who lives in the kitchen immediately issued an excited babble of instructions, and housewives flew off in all directions and brought so much furniture you can't get from one side of the little room to another without an alpenstock.

The lady who lives with her seven children in the apartment directly above has just come back with the children in tow to tell me she remembers something she forgot to tell me. In addition to her uncle in Pittsburgh, she also has a second cousin in Des Moines, Iowa. She's gone upstairs to get his picture.

With the 8th Army in Italy (September 26, 1943)

Twenty-seven hours before they evacuated this Italian town, German soldiers forced twenty-one male civilians to kneel before a firing squad outside a local cemetery. Twenty of the civilians were killed instantly by a point-blank fusillade from machine-guns, light automatics, rifles and pistols. The twenty-first escaped by playing dead.

The men were rounded up at random and executed within thirty minutes of the killing of a local farmer who had shot a German soldier in the hands while attempting to prevent the Nazi from stealing a chicken.

Today I saw twelve of the bloated, bullet-riddled corpses lying in wooden coffins in the cemetery, while forty yards away a party of fellow-citizens dug the deep hole that was to be their common grave. I saw the place of execution, with the ground crusted with clots of hardened blood.

I talked to the man who knelt to meet his death and lived by a miracle.

I attended the funeral wake of one of the victims and talked with scores of people who saw them go to their fate.

I read a copy of the public proclamation in which the German commandant admitted fifteen of the killings.

This is not an "atrocity" story. It is a factual record.

The Germans left Rionero, a farming town of ten thousand population, last night. At four o'clock the day before yesterday a group of German soldiers accompanied by four Italian parachutists still fighting on the side of the Nazis entered the yard of Pasquale Sibilia, a middle-aged farmer. Sibilia's little daughter Elena ran into the house crying, "Papa! They are stealing our chickens!"

With seven children to feed and food growing shorter, Sibilia remonstrated in a way that a terrorized Italian seldom dares to remonstrate against German pillage. He argued futilely. Then he went back into the house, brought out a rifle and shot one of the Germans in the hand.

Sibilia was killed at once before the eyes of his family. Then the Germans and their four Italian companions dispersed through near-by streets, gathering in boys and men at the points of their guns. Until just before the last, many victims thought they were being drafted for a forced labour detail. None of them resisted.

They were marched through the streets to where the road winds past a high shoulder. They were ordered to kneel, facing the road. Then, without further warning, the execution squad of fourteen Germans and four Italians opened fire on them. The first bursts killed all but four of the twenty-one. Three others were finished off with pistol fire. The fourth, Stefano di Mattia, twenty-one-year-old bricklayer, was overlooked. Some bullet had grazed his leg. He lay still among his dead companions until long after the Germans had gone.

The news spread quickly through the town's shocked homes. Everyone in Rionero had a son, a husband, a father or a friend in that sprawling red pile of corpses on the hillside, but when sobbing mothers and wives went to reclaim their dead they were driven away. The corpses were to be burned, they were told.

But with Allied patrols already skirting the town, the German garrison of between fifty and a hundred men withdrew last night without making the slightest attempt to hide the evidence of their crime. Troops did tear down the proclamation in which it was admitted officially that "there have already been killed fifteen men who were responsible for having fired against a German soldier," but not before copies had been made by civilians.

Stefano di Mattia, the man who lived through the swift but horrible nightmare, led me and another correspondent through the mourning town and showed us the brown patch of earth where he had knelt less than forty-eight hours previously with his twenty friends, and then took us to the cemetery.

Eight of the bodies already had been buried. The other twelve were piled in their coffins two deep in the graveyard's little mortuary. Silently the gravediggers laid the blood-stained, swollen shapes in a row so that military photographers could add the final testimony of the camera.

The oldest there was Antonio di Passo, thirty-five-year-old farmer, and the youngest was Marco Greco, a sixteen-year-old salesman's apprentice. Outside the cemetery gates a lonely knot of women and children waited while the work of preparing the graves proceeded.

Allied soldiers who entered Rionero today behind the retreating Germans dare not guess what is happening further ahead. At dawn today an Italian soldier came to the front from Melfi, twelve kilometres beyond Rionero. He carried a note which read: "My dearest comrades, my wife and my daughter yesterday have been killed by the Germans. Now I will fight with you against the Germans."

Beside this man's story, the story of Rionero seems commonplace. His is a story of mass-murder, mutilation and assault on women and children that eclipsed the worst part of the German record in Poland and Russia. It can't be told without direct verification.

Whether the next few days produces this verification or not, those of us who have seen what happened in one Italian town cannot be surprised by anything the Germans may do in other towns.

PRESS CONFERENCE

London (March 18, 1944)

That flourishing wartime institution, the press conference, has been described as a gathering at which a person who knows everything meets a group of people who think they know everything and tells them nothing in the strictest confidence.

This is harsh. It is true that the press conference has expanded faster than almost any other branch of industry, and that an instrument of public information which used to be considered the property of Prime Ministers and Presidents has been eagerly embraced by hundreds of lesser officials.

It is true that many busy administrators have become so steeped in the press conference habit that they often hold conferences whether they have anything to say or not. It is true that most newspapermen will be happy when the vogue passes, and they are free again to stalk their news sources independently, every man for himself and page twenty-seven take the hindmost.

But it is also true that the press conference has certain attractions and attributes which cannot be gauged by any printer's measure; for instance, it is fine morale.

Brendan Bracken's conferences are particularly good for morale. The Minister of Information sits before a bare mahogany desk chain-feeding himself cigarettes and talks for about an hour, in a low, confidential voice, about all subjects in which his audience expresses an interest. Mr. Bracken is usually as frank as it's safe to be, and it isn't until they're back in their offices that it begins to occur to his listeners that they haven't heard very much that they haven't already read in the *Times*.

Mr. Bracken normally breaks out a bottle of Scotch after these mass interviews. Mr. Bracken's admirers consider that this action reflects a praiseworthy grasp of the temper of the Fourth Estate in these anxious times, and frequently compare it, to the latter institution's disadvantage, with the Foreign Office custom of serving tea and seed-cake.

There are elements of adventure in all press conferences. You never know when you might meet an unannounced celebrity.

At one conference they had a Cabinet Minister, a full general and jam tart.

At another conference, held recently in Italy, a group of veteran 8th Army correspondents were invited to meet a visiting Russian general. The meeting developed into something of a reunion, for the Russian general turned out to be the same man who had followed the 8th Army from Alamein to Mareth as war correspondent for Pravda. He had been a general then, too, he explained urbanely to the astonished English authors, although he hadn't thought it worth mentioning at the time.

Military press conferences, of course, are indispensable, for it is through the correlated intelligence reports from the various sectors of the front which are read there that correspondents working out of general headquarters and army headquarters are enabled to prepare the general news leads that supplement the front-line stories.

At Algiers the daily "sitrep" – for situation report – is issued around noon by an Army public-relations officer, who stands at one end of a long rectangular room facing a roomful of sixty to eighty expectant typewriters and explains each point as he makes it by referring to a large wall map.

Mostly the Algiers conference is as casual and unwarlike as a class in geometry, although it has its moments of drama, as, for example, the day a new officer was placed in charge and, suddenly overwhelmed at finding himself the sole repository of a fistful of world secrets, replied to a tricky question on some phase of the day's fighting by clearing his throat solemnly and announcing: "Off the record, I don't know."

Two of the unluckiest press conferences ever held in the Mediterranean Theatre were both conducted by the same man, a high-ranking officer of the Royal Air Force. One morning last August he told a party of correspondents encamped near the Lentini airfield: "The *Luftwaffe* is finished in this area. So long as you stay here, you will never see another German plane."

Late the same night the authors scrambled out of their bed rolls in time to see the *Luftwaffe* finish a tidy raid on the adjoining airfield in which more than thirty of our grounded planes were destroyed or damaged.

Four months later the same officer said at another press conference in Bari: "If a single German plane came over here, I should take it as a personal insult." A few hours later the Germans staged the attack in which seventeen Allied ships were sunk in Bari harbour.

Probably the leading example of press-conference confidence which has yet come out of this war was manifested at a special conference held in London immediately after Dunkirk. Most of the authors attending had been back in England only a few hours after scrambling across the Channel as best they could in the full rush of that almost fatal defeat. A titled general met them in the conference-room to fulfil that traditional press-conference function known as "explaining the broader background."

"After all, gentlemen," the peer began in the utmost earnestness, "our army has nothing to worry about. The records show that in the entiah German General Staff there is not one general who held a rank highah than colonel in the lawst war."

On the whole the people who give press conferences seldom provide half as much entertainment as the people who attend them. Newspaper people are notorious for their egotism and allied peculiarities, and there's always at least one reporter in every gathering who is far less interested in finding out how much the big guy at the front of the room knows than in letting the big guy know how much he knows himself.

A more spectacular type of *habitué* is the chronic woolgatherer, who periodically comes out of a trance to ask a question that the interlocutor has just spent twelve manful minutes attempting to answer.

The local champion is an elderly lady journalist, widely respected for her years and sex, and her reputation is founded in part, although not wholly, on a performance she gave at a conference presided over by Ernest Bevin, the Minister of Labour.

Mr. Bevin was having difficulty justifying certain aspects of his labour policy to a critical audience. The Minister was showing visible signs of impatience. His audience was being respectful but somewhat testily dogged. Suddenly, in the midst of a charged silence the lady journalist turned her head from the window from which she had evidently been studying some phase of bird life in a near-by park, and said, in her sweetest and most ringing tones, just to keep the conversation from dragging: "Mr. Bevin, isn't it wonderful how we in the Empire are standing together?"

Readers of these despatches sometimes complain that there's not enough news in them. My only reply is that I have no time to gather news. I'm too busy attending press conferences.

SLEEPLESS AND HUNGRY CANADIANS SLUG AHEAD

With the Canadians in France (June 7, 1944)

Land fighting on the Canadian frontage is still severe. The general area is a deep coastal strip hinged on a chain of little resort villages on the Channel. Their streets run to tidy hedge-rows, houses and avenues of lime trees, beech, pine and poplar. The fields beyond are flat and well cultivated. The people are poor, but it is nothing like the utter endless peasant poverty which the soldiers met in rural Italy. There are few signs here of hunger, and fewer signs of that cloying servility of the spirit which followed the Fascist collapse in Italy. Here the people are proud and independent. Most of them, incidentally, appear to be fervent de Gaullists.

France will doubtless become a land of romantic memory for the soldiers of General Eisenhower, but up to now most of the troops have been far too busy with the immediate problems of killing Germans, and preventing Germans from killing them, to conduct anything but the most cursory check of Uncle Edgar's version of extramilitary culture in this part of the world.

It is now two nights and days since the last of the invasion army sailed from England, and anyone who can truthfully say he has had more than two scratchy meals or two hours of cold, cramped sleep is either one of the wounded or one of the Lord's chosen.

The weather hasn't been good to us. It started off by creating a sea-swell that drenched the whole assault force to the armpits and continued its unfriendly caprices last night by covering a golden moon with a blanket of clouds, thus encouraging the *Luftwaffe* to make gingerly raids on our beaches and supply lines from 11 P.M. onward.

There was low overcast cloud still hanging over the coast at daybreak, delaying the enemy air forces' full retreat before the day fighters arrived. The German raids appeared to be only of token dimensions and did little damage, but they impelled an almost continuous ack-ack barrage from the Allied invasion fleet lying off shore. It was spectacular, noisy and highly comforting, but anything but conducive to rest.

Between watches soldiers out on patrol or other immediate combat duties shivered in clammy slit trenches, some with one blanket for cover, some with only thin rubberized gas-capes.

The only members of the invasion force who got a real night's sleep were ten carrier pigeons who came ashore with the public relations detachment, but are temporarily excused from military duty.

The chances are in this war that the Allied troops will get along even better with the French than Uncle Edgar claimed to get along with them, but, as they slug ahead in what promises to be a war of movement with a vengeance, there isn't likely to be much time for renewing the vintage amenities of the First Great War. What wine the Germans haven't already stolen or bought at their own prices is still lying in secret vaults or burial grounds, the inhabitants say as they apologetically offer lemonade and water.

It's true that the first troops were handed red roses by *mesdemoiselles* who looked almost as nice as those Uncle Edgar used to talk about, but any gratuitous embraces that may have been kicking around this part of France have been contributed by pappa and mamma.

A dreamy young Canadian captain put this side of the international relations situation in a wistful nutshell when he described his own first contact with the civilian population.

"I could see there were some pretty girls peeking out from behind the hedges as I marched down the street," the captain said, "but none of them seemed to be very interested in me. Suddenly, from just behind my right ear, I heard a husky whisper 'I love you.' I turned around quick and there was an old man of at least seventy-five."

It was only when he started thinking about his high-school

43

languages that the captain remembered that the French make no distinction between the words for "like" and "love."

TWILIGHT OF YOUTH

With the Canadians in France (July 9, 1944)

In the tortured wreckage of Caen, British and Canadian soldiers today were bearing bloody witness to the twilight of the Hitler *Jugend*.

The 12th ss Panzer Division was the final flowering of the original Adolf Hitler Youth, the boys of six and seven years who began to drill with tiny wooden rifles and parade in goose-step when the Nazis came to power in 1933. Today the 12th ss Panzer is a division no more. Its living remnants are still fighting in pockets outside the suburbs, but these living remnants are far outnumbered by the dead. They lie where they fell yesterday in the levelled streets of Authie, Buron, Gruchy, Cussy, Ardenne, Franqueville, in splintered orchards and in acre after acre of grain fields where this year's only harvest will be a harvest of soaked slit trenches and weapon pits.

Beside them are their live grenades and the blackened hulks of their tanks.

A few have surrendered. A few have broken under the relentless onslaught of these last thirty-six hours and have become suddenly the little boys they never gave themselves a chance to be. But for the most part the pride of the Hitler Youth has died.

You hear a lot about the Fascist soldier who fights with maniacal or fanatic or suicidal fury. These are the words that must be used to describe the way the sullen, beardless striplings of the 12th ss Panzers have fought since yesterday at dawn. An hour ago a Canadian corporal said of them "they look like babies and they die like mad bastards."

The colonel of a Canadian infantry battalion led me through the terrible debris of a part of yesterday's battlefield where his battalion was forming up to push on again. He pointed to a burnt-out Sherman tank and not fifteen yards away a wrecked German 75-mm. gun.

"This will give you a rough idea what fighting these people is like," the colonel said. "These Germans sat on their gun-belly down in the wheat until the tank was on top of them. They let go.

They got the tank and, of course, they were killed themselves a few minutes afterwards."

Throughout yesterday's tumultuous battle, the last of the Hitler Youth sat under two barrages, their own and ours, waiting for Canadian infantrymen to push on beyond their carefully concealed snipers' nests and machine-gun posts in the fields. Then, after deliberately allowing themselves to be surrounded, they would fire on the backs of leading Canadian troops, exact as high a price as they could, and then die in a spitting hail of Stens, pistols and grenades.

Often they "played dead," and allowed the first rush of our infantry charge to speed right over them.

"I was going through a nasty piece of mortaring when I looked down into a trench and saw an apparently dead German with the muzzle of his pistol jammed in his mouth," Major A.J. Wilson, Charlottetown, said. "Just as I went past I saw his eyes roll. I made a lunge for him, and he pulled the trigger. All these people have been told that they'll be shot if they're taken prisoner. This kid apparently was working on his last bullet."

Major Harry Anderson, Kitchener, company commander in an Ontario regiment that battled the 12th ss Panzers through the thickest of yesterday's fighting, told of meeting a nest of Germans as he and his batman, Private Peter Barbeck, Windsor, worked their way through a meadow. Private Barbeck spotted the Germans first. They were in a trench. One of them jumped out at Barbeck, tugged at a pin on a hand grenade, and fired a wild burst from his tommy gun. Major Anderson and Private Barbeck got grenades away almost simultaneously and the enemy pocket was erased.

"This is one redeeming feature of fighting these madmen," Major Anderson said. "They sometimes get excited and miss set-up targets."

Major Art Sparks, Woodstock, Ont., a member of the same unit, saw another German youngster step into the blazing machine guns of a Sherman tank to fire an anti-tank hand mortar from twenty feet away. He missed, too, in his wild-eyed excitement.

Another German Sparks told about held out in a slit trench, catching Canadian grenades and throwing them back before they exploded. Finally one blew his right arm off. He threw another back with his left hand before he missed one and was instantly killed.

45

Normandy (August 2, 1944)

Question: Is it true the French are apathetic, and sometimes hostile to their liberators?

New arrivals from England usually begin by asking this question, and at least one of them rushed back to London within twenty-four hours and wrote out his own answer. The fact that the answer, a vitriolic condemnation of the French, was silly, is largely beside the point. The question itself is silly.

A Frenchwoman searching through the ruins of her home for the body of her baby is almost certain to look apathetic to any one who believes that she ought to look either apathetic or pleased – one thing or the other, and no hedging. She might even look hostile to a person who believes there is no room in such cases for shades and degrees of feeling.

The truth as I see it – and after only seven weeks here I am only beginning to realize how hard it is to arrive at the truth – is that the French, who have every excuse for misunderstanding us, have been teaching us, who have no excuse for misunderstanding them, a great lesson in patience and native wisdom.

The cost the Allied armies have paid for this foothold in Normandy is not less than the cost the French have paid to make room for it in the blighted acres of their farms and the stinking wreckage of their homes. In lives, our cost has been greater than theirs. But we have had this one edge on them: we always knew what it would be like; we knew within reasonable bounds what the casualties would be and how they would be inflicted. The French didn't know what it would be like, didn't know what the casualties would be, and expected that such casualties as they might have to accept would be inflicted by the arms of their enemies, the Germans. The last real war they had in this part of Normandy was a simple, old-fashioned religious war in the seventeenth century. In that kind of war your enemies shot you up, your friends protected you, and there wasn't the slightest excuse for confusing one with the other.

But if there ever was a predisposition among the Normans of this war to confuse their friends with their enemies, the last seven weeks have given it every excuse for taking a firm and even militant hold. Scores of their towns have been levelled. Even in the towns that have escaped lightly their six and seven hundred-year-old churches have been demolished one by one, because churches always make the best observation posts. Caen, Normandy's finest city after Rouen, was virtually flattened without warning and between two and three thousand people who had remained there to welcome the Allies were buried in the ruins.

Yet no percentage of these people worth speaking of has confused effect with cause or cause with motive. The cause is not the British bomber, but the German panzer that rolled in four years ago. The motive is not to destroy the French home, but to destroy the German who uses it for a fort. We know this well enough, but they might well be forgiven for forgetting it. They haven't forgotten, even while they have buried their dead.

Perhaps one tenth of one per cent have been actively unfriendly. At first a few thought we had only come for another Dieppe, and were careful not to jeopardize their standing with the Germans. A few women had formed formal or informal alliances with German soldiers. Among the merchants a few saw liberation as an opportunity to jack up their prices. Among the politicians a few saw it only as the cue for hauling down the Swastika and running up the Union Jack. These are representative human beings, but it isn't fair to call them representative Frenchmen. If, to draw a long and by no means funny analogy, the Germans happened to occupy Canada and the Yanks came after four years to drive them out, the Yanks would undoubtedly find a few Canadian women who had been living with German soldiers, a few respectable merchants offering to sell the liberators beer at a dollar and a half a bottle, and a few politicians lining up to explain why they had found it in the public interest to collaborate with the Germans.

These would be representative human beings too, but not representative Canadians.

The enveloping majority of Frenchmen and Frenchwomen have behaved as gallantly and understandingly and steadfastly as any Canadian could hope that Canadian men and women would behave in parallel circumstances. To the first liberating troops they have extended as warm a welcome as they could – sometimes wine, sometimes flowers, more often only a sad smile and a wave of the hand. Then they have gone about their business, the heartsick business of hunting for their families or for bread and shelter. There isn't time to stand and wave at everybody.

A soldier seeing their faces from the back of a supply truck, ten days after the front has passed, can't always tell what cause the faces have to be sober. If the soldier sees a frown he can't always tell that it may only be the perplexed frown of a man who is still wondering whether his wife will turn up yet by some miracle, in a hospital he has not yet heard about.

The people haven't complained. In seven weeks, except for a child's occasional request for chocolate, the only thing I have been asked for is permission to listen to a radio. The people of Normandy have retained their self-sufficiency along with their self-respect and dignity. They have been our friends and hundreds of them have sealed the friendship with their lives. Until there is some way of proving that any people anywhere could have borne themselves with greater fortitude and good-will under a comparable weight of suffering, the question of their so-called "apathy" would be better left in abeyance.

NOTABLE SIGHTS AND SOUNDS IN A WAR-FILLED COUNTRY

With the Canadians in France (August 7, 1944)

The memories pile up fast, and most of them will be unpleasant. But in two places in Brittany today, three new ones bubbled up from the turgid depths of another day of war, like spring water rising from the bed of a volcano. These three memories will be worth hanging on to.

One was a smell. It came off a sun-lit field beside a road that by some freak no one apparently had thought of using to carry military traffic. There was not a vehicle, live or dead, on the road. There were no tank-tracks or shell-scars in the field. The farmhouses around had the whole and healthy look of farmhouses on a 1938 postcard. There was no cordite in the air, no smoke, no scent of charred wood or broken stone baked in naked flame. No petrol fumes or dust, no dead cows or horses, not even dead men. When the breeze drifted down from the field across the road, it carried only the smell of new-mown hay.

Another memory was a sound. In a side street café in a town from which the Germans had departed only twelve hours before, the patroness gave us omelettes and white wine for lunch. As we ate, the patroness' four-year-old daughter came in and stood in front of another table on which there was a tiny piano. With two chubby fingers, the little girl picked out a tuneless chord for herself, and then, poking a tuneless accompaniment, sang gravely in a high thin treble voice that might have belonged to almost any little girl. The song could have belonged only to a little girl in France, who, until twelve hours before, had never been allowed to sing it in public. It began "Allons enfants de la patrie." When she finished, the little girl walked gravely back into the kitchen, pretending she had not known anyone was listening.

The third memory was a discussion. Three boys came into the café, each wearing the brassard of the Maquis on his arm, and each carrying a bayonet in his belt. The eldest of the three, who might have been sixteen, also carried a German Schmeizer machine gun. The three boys said they had been shooting and capturing Germans for the last two days, and probably they had, for the Maquis of Brittany sprang to arms quickly and violently when the Americans turned into the peninsula.

The boys, trying to sound as though they had been drinking that haymaker of the applejack family all their lives, ordered Calvados. "Calvados, indeed!" the patroness shrilled. Then she gave the young Maquis a stern lecture on the subject of boys who attempt to handle drinks that are safe for only the strongest men. The patroness told them never to ask her for Calvados again, and said if they ever did she would tell their mothers.

The three boys slunk out, crestfallen. When they reached the street, they squared their shoulders again and walked toward the outskirts of the town to see if they could find any more Germans. They were still old enough for that.

A BLACK AND THUNDEROUS NIGHTMARE:
CANADIANS BOMBED BY 500 RAF PLANES

With the Canadian First Army in France (August 14, 1944)

Hundreds of soldiers of the Canadian 1st Army today experienced the last refinement of total war – a full-scale attack by the four-motored heavies of the Royal Air Force's Bomber Command.

For periods ranging from a few minutes to the full hour and five minutes it took to call off an attack by more than seven hundred bombers that had somehow gone astray, troops as much as four miles behind the target areas felt the full weight of the most devastating weapon in military history.

Many were killed and many others wounded. Some were shell-shocked. Even those who were still unscathed after the last of an estimated five hundred Allied bomb loads had been dropped inside the Canadian lines were badly shaken as they emerged from reeking shell craters, dugouts and slit trenches into scenes filled with the smoke of their burning supply dumps and the noise and flame of exploding ammunition lorries. Most of them took what consolation they could by reminding themselves that what Allied soldiers had just experienced for the first time, German soldiers and war workers are experiencing every day.

In the black and thunderous nightmare, I sat in a quaking dugout with twenty Canadian soldiers, waiting for the direct hit that would almost certainly have obliterated us all. We were in a stone quarry near Hautemesnil, a village on the Caen-Falaise Road, two and a half miles above the German positions against which the mammoth air raid was directed.

The bombing reached its saturation point there and continued with short intervals of grace from 3 to 3:44 PM.

The dividing lines between nervousness and fear and between fear and terror sometimes become so thin in battle that I will not attempt to define my feelings. But whatever it was like sitting under the crashing English and Canadian bombs, I know I have never known anything like it before.

My personal chamber of horrors from this war had previously included German and Italian bombs of several sizes and varieties. Moaning Minnie and her little sisters, the German bullets, rocket guns, 88-mm. field guns and 15 and 17 centimetre mediums.

Beyond recording that everybody else in the dugout behaved magnificently, the only further light I can throw on the question "How does it feel to be bombed by the RAF?" is to say I think my head was clear, but when I left the dugout I was wringing wet from head to toe; that I did not pray, but would have prayed had I not felt it would be presumptuous; that I never ceased to hope I would get out alive and never ceased to suspect that I would not.

From the top of the quarry, H.D. Zeiman, correspondent of the *Daily Telegraph,* Collin Rayment, from Montreal, our conducting officer, and I watched the first squadron of Lancasters come in, two hours after the Canadian infantry had launched an attack across the Laison River toward Falaise, and drop their bombs with perfect accuracy in the area of Quesney Wood, two and a half miles from our observation post.

Soon the target area was virtually obliterated with leaping towers of smoke and at twenty minutes to three, forty minutes after the first bombs had dropped, we decided to walk down to a shelf of the quarry to a brigade headquarters and see what information we could pick up there about progress of the ground operations.

Before we reached our destination it had already become apparent that something had suddenly gone wrong with the bombing program. British heavies had changed their course slightly and when we heard the next gargantuan blast of heavy bombs and saw the next pillar of smoke belch toward the sky, the area had somehow shifted to our own lines. Bombs appeared to fall on Cauvicourt, a mile northeast of the quarry.

Brigade headquarters was already reporting it to division when we arrived at the operations room, a dugout that had served as a German divisional headquarters only a few days before.

The officers and men around the headquarters were looking anxiously across the road and some of them were giving voice to sympathetic "damns" for the supply troops and gun crews we knew were operating over there. It always is a sobering thing to see bombs come down on friend *or* foe. But even then this didn't look like anything worse than an incident in the central tragedy of war. It looked at worst as though one squadron had lost its way. The others, we assured ourselves, would hit the beam again. The major who was on duty at the operations room invited us to walk a hundred yards to his trench and there he poured us a drink of lemonade.

While we were drinking the lemonade another stick of bombs fell across the road just south of Cauvicourt. We put down our glasses and everybody started saying "damn". We weren't damning anything much but luck or fate, as a person damns luck or fate when he hears of the death of a friend. We could hear ammunition exploding across the road now amid the heavy, wracking spasms of bomb explosions and we knew for sure that men were dying over there. It hadn't occurred to anybody at the brigade headquarters that the headquarters itself was in danger.

But the next wave of bombers hit due north of us and it occurred to us that perhaps it was time to take note of the fact that bombs had now been dropped on three sides of us and that there were hundreds more planes still in the air coming straight toward us. The planes were flying low. We waited another minute, looking through our binoculars to see if the bomb doors on the leading planes were open. Then the major called out: "Everybody in trenches or dugouts."

Private Jerome Latour, Toronto, driver of our press jeep, jumped in and drove the jeep along the quarry shelf to the front of the dugout, where there was protection for it to one side. Rayment, Zeiman, the major and I jogged along on foot glancing uneasily over our shoulders, but we made it just as the first bomb hit the quarry with the deafening, teeth-shattering impact of a rabbit-punch from a giant. We spilled inside the dugout, past a narrow runway, down two steps and around a corner into a square room in which eight or ten privates were already sitting around a kerosene lamp.

There wasn't much to the room but a big operations map and a double tier of wooden bunks. The soldiers moved back on the bunks to make room. One of them sat on a box, his head bent over a set of signaller's earphones. "Hello, Sarah Two, Hello Sarah Two, we are being bombed. Over," he was saying. His voice was firm, clear and decidedly matter of fact.

The rabbit-punches were raining down by now, and through the smoke-filled corridor of the dugout every now and then the hot, liquid fingers of a blast reached and tugged as though to drag us out of our trembling haven by sheer force.

We had now become the preferred target. The bombs came at us in retching sticks and each time a stick started we held our breaths and covered our heads with our arms. Theoretically, this latter operation was calculated to save our eyes, and possibly our heads; speaking for myself, it was simply the ostrich complex at work. The major ordered the light put out and imposed a ban on smoking.

The third stick, I think it was, knocked down the wall map, tore loose the ends of two firmly nailed two-by-six planks at the entrance to the inner room and showered a large amount of loose dirt on us. I counted one hundred bombs that fell within what I judged to be an area of a hundred yards of the dugout.

Between waves we debated whether it would be better to make a dash for the lower part of the quarry where there were deep caves. Some of us got outside, but were driven back by exploding ammunition. The whole quarry was a cauldron of smoke and flame and crazily whining and spluttering shells meant for the breeches of our medium and field guns.

One batch of small-arms ammunition was going up just beyond the shelf like a machine-gun barrage. It was well for us that we were driven back into the dugout. We later learned that in the narrow caves below, the blast was taking a heavy toll of casualties. Anyway, the bombers were back before we could have made the caves.

The signaller was still at work with his earphones. "Hello, Sarah Two. Hello, Sarah Two. We are being bombed. Over." Somebody near the front of the dugout said: "Tell them by our own bombs." "Hello, Sarah Two," the signaller said. "We are being bombed by our own planes, own planes. Over." "I can't get any answer," the signaller said, "but nearly everybody on the line is reporting the same thing."

Another soldier groped down from the front of the dugout with the help of a flashlight. "It's no use trying to make them hear you," he said. "Your transformers have been knocked out." The bombers were coming in so low we could hear their motors long before we heard their bombs. When another batch rolled in one of the soldiers on the bed said:

"I hope they go for somebody else for a change."

"Shut up," another voice said in the dark.

"It helps to talk," the first soldier said aggrievedly.

"Shut up anyway," the second soldier said.

There was a radio receiver going in the little hallway, pouring a mixture of static and shrill, whining jazz into the thumping overture of the bombs. The dugout became thick with smoke and powder-fumes. When I covered my head with my hand my hands came away wet.

We did our best to listen to the radio, which, in quick succession, gave us Bing Crosby in "Going My Way" and "Would You Rather be a Mule?"

And then a very wonderful thing happened. A BBC announcer succeeded Crosby and, speaking with the authoritative aloofness that is the exclusive property of BBC announcers, said that Bomber Command was at this very minute bombing enemy targets near Falaise and doing so with complete success. In our shivering dugout the crisp bulletin provoked some fairly robust comment.

At sixteen minutes to four the last bomb was dropped on the quarry. After the longest lull of the whole interlude the major said:

"We have only ten more minutes to go. Four o'clock's the deadline."

It was a long ten minutes, longer than the forty-five minutes during which the bombs had been dropping on the quarry. It was another twenty minutes before we could go outside. Our jeep lay two inches thick in dust, two tires blown and its engine smashed beside an eight-foot-deep bomb crater just at the entrance to the dugout. The other craters in the area varied up to thirty feet in width. We hitch-hiked home after swinging low along the shoulders of the quarry for protection against the ammunition that was still spluttering below.

For a mile and a half by a mile and a half the entire Canadian area seemed to be in smoke but the ambulances were streaming in among the craters, taking the wounded back.

NORMANDY TALES

Chartres (August 19, 1944)

The road to Paris is a road that Chaucer would have loved. Its clean, beflagged and miraculously whole borders are peopled with the brave and fair, and with the weak, the tired and the guilty. As the armed columns race on through Laval, Le Mans, Nogent and Chartres they see little but the endless miles of waving hands and the endless ripple of flags.

Those of us who are able to stop see just enough to make us wish the man who wrote the *Canterbury Tales* about another highway could be here to write the story of Highways 157, 23, 22 and 29 the way it should be written. Here, at any rate, are some of the people Chaucer would have written about on the road to Paris.

The Housewife: Most of the country between Laval and Chartres has been free for between one and two weeks. But still in the intermediate towns and villages there is scarcely a doorway in which a woman doesn't stand as though keeping vigil, waving to each individual lorry, jeep or tank, even when the vehicles are crowded nose to tail.

Between the villages under majestic avenues of Lombardy poplars, chestnuts and plane trees, the women sit in the grass beside the road knitting, with their fresh-scrubbed children playing beside them. The children make the v sign, and when a soldier returns the salute the children's faces are radiant with accomplishment and pride.

There is such an orgy of waving here that you suspect the people have heard echoes of reproach from Normandy, where some of our follow-up troops took it as a sign of indifference that the waving stopped after two or three days. Here the most out-distanced supply lorry, the rearmost echelon of the rearmost formation, and the most belated newspaper jeep is greeted as enthusiastically as though its occupants were the unaided libera-tors of all France.

The Slave Labourer: Just outside Le Mans marching against the traffic there were four groups of women, four abreast, striding out in perfect, long-swinging paces. All were bareheaded, some were barefooted. Their costumes ranged from faded black Sunday dresses to blue men's overalls. As our jeep passed each group, the broad, strong faces smiled as one, and thick, muscular arms shot up the salute of the clenched fist.

These were *"les femmes Russes,"* on the way to work in the fields as volunteers. Since April they had been working as con-scripts for the German *Todt* labour organization, repairing rail-roads and building supply shelters. There were two hundred and twenty of them in all. Some had been captured in battle fighting as soldiers of the Red Army. Some had been taken in guerrilla war-fare. Others had been rounded up as political suspects and still more on no better grounds than that they were strong enough to do the work of men. Their ages ran from fourteen to seventy-three.

In the wire-enclosed square of their wooden barracks we talked to their "chief," Maria Volkoff of Pushkin, near Leningrad. Madame Volkoff told us the Russian women had at first been required to work ten hours a day with one full Sunday and three half Sundays off each month. Their pay was eight francs an hour, but compulsory deductions for food, clothing and soap cut the average monthly net wage to between three and four hundred francs – six to eight dollars. As the military situation became more urgent, working conditions for the Russian women became progressively worse. Near the end they worked fourteen hours a day, seven days a week. Their German "overseers" carried clubs and beat the women, frequently without provocation.

Madame Volkoff told her story without emotion until she spoke of her own family. Her husband was dead when the Ger-mans came to Pushkin. When the Germans took Madame Volkoff to a concentration camp without specifying any charge against her, she left her seventy-six-year-old mother and one-year-old son together and homelesss. Madame Volkoff has heard nothing of either. As she told us this tears coursed down her strong peasant face and she reproached herself bitterly. "It is not worthy of a Russian woman to cry," she said.

The Patriot: He wore a thin blue polo-shirt, a pair of grey slacks, and high on his knotted right arm was the brassard of the Maquis. He had the broad, slightly protruding Joe-E.-Brown-lips that are peculiar to a certain factory class in France, and the lips were folded back in a smile of sheer delight.

It was past the closing hour for dinner, but the patron personally served the patriot with the best aperitif in the house. Conversation stopped, and every one knew he had been on a mission and would soon talk about it.

He told it between great gusts of laughter and profane, joyous bangings on the table with his huge fist. The café rocked with laughter. War is not a happy thing, but if there are any happy warriors in France they are to be found among the Maquis.

The Collaborationist: Perhaps it is unfair to call him that. The evidence is that he served too long and too well as mayor of the village while the Germans were there. When the French Forces of the Interior drove the Germans out in a street-battle one of the first things they did was to inform the mayor politely that his services were no longer needed. The mayor accepted their decision. He did what he thought was best for the village, he says.

Collaborationist or not, the ex-mayor's political views were sufficient credentials to give him a forty-five-minute interview with Marshall Pétain two years ago. This interview remains the high moment of his life. He exhibits the picture he had taken beside Pétain with great pride.

"There is no mystery about Pétain," he says frankly. "Pétain simply does not like the English. He did not like them in 1914."

The Middle-of-the-Roader: He was editor of a weekly paper. The paper missed one issue while the fighting was going on, then it resumed publication with the same size and format.

The editorial content differed sharply. In the issue of August 5, the last issue under the Germans, the German *communiqué* occupied the upper left-hand corner and the leading news story was a highly coloured report of the activities of a number of French "terrorists" and "bandits."

In the issue of August 19 the Allied *communiqué* was featured and the top news story was about liberation of the village by the French Forces of the Interior. There was a half-column-long obituary for two patriots who had lost their lives in the fighting between the resistance forces and the Germans.

We asked the editor if the patriots and the liberators of whom he wrote in his August 19 paper were not the same people as the terrorists and bandits of whom he had written on August 5. He admitted there was a strong likelihood that we were right. But obviously, he indicated, this was no concern of his. He had written what the Germans made him write. If his conscience ever troubled him he had no difficulty in conquering it.

The Returned Soldier: Five times he had escaped from the Germans, this young Frenchman. The fifth time he was caught right on the old line of demarcation between Occupied France and Vichy France.

The sixth time he came all the way from the Ukraine through the heart of Germany and reached his home three days after it had been freed by the Americans.

The Flag-Dealer: He was unable to supply us with a Tricolour, and he said sadly that we will be unable to buy one anywhere this side of Paris.

"I was in Paris two weeks ago to buy what flags I could," he said. "Their manufacture is forbidden but there are factories working underground. Alas, they cannot begin to meet the demand. I smuggled out as many flags as they could sell me. Until Paris is freed I will get no more."

THE LIBERATION OF PARIS

Paris (August 26, 1944)

Paris today is Betty Grable on a bicycle and Billy the Kid on a bender. Paris is the Mona Lisa in a jeep and François Villon behind a Sten gun. Paris is all the people in the world packed into the biggest parade that was ever held. Paris is all the flags and all the singing, all the waves and all the cheers.

Paris is all the bullets hammering loud against the grey stone walls of the Grand Boulevard and all the ambulances and fire-engines racing God knows where. Paris is all the beauty and the bravery and all the fine high-soaring hopes.

Paris is De Gaulle standing bareheaded beneath the Arc de Triomphe and an old woman crying softly in the Place de la Concorde.

Tomorrow – or the day after at the very most – Paris will begin to face its future of hardship and hunger. But today, on Saturday, August 26, it was so magic and incredible a place that only a child dreaming a child's golden, half-troubled dreams on the night before Christmas could imagine what it looked like.

Paris today was partly itself at its best, partly Deadwood Gulch at its worst and partly Strauss' Vienna at its most improbable.

I have just been through a sweaty milling and I have no hesitancy in admitting I had an anxious hour of ambush in the Rue de Rivoli, and as I sit typing this despatch in a sinfully luxurious suite in the Ritz Hotel bullets are splattering on the walls of the courtyard not fifty feet away. Like all the shooting in Paris today there is nothing much you can do about it but ignore it. And besides, as the last incipient movie actress who kissed me (forcibly, honey, I swear) expressed it: "Why let a little shooting spoil a day like this?"

The day began modestly enough. After a riotous ride through the suburbs Friday afternoon, my travelling companion and I spent a relatively quiet night in a little hotel in Montparnasse. There was a good deal of shooting, but by morning it had died down and in Montparnasse the mood of the morning of the first day of freedom was the soberly happy but anxious mood which, after the heady effervescence of the celebration has died away, will turn out, after all, to have been the more lasting mood of a city that is still not clear of tragedy.

People lined up almost at dawn for bread. They read the papers – the first free papers the youngest of them had ever read – with sober, anxious faces. Almost everyone, it seemed, had a relative or a close friend to ask about. Did we know so and so in Canada, and so and so in the United States or England? When would it be possible to write letters?

When and how the eminently practical mind in which Paris began its first day of liberation came to change can only be a subject for speculation. Perhaps it was because the news spread that the German Military Commandant of Paris, General von Choltitz, had surrendered to General Leclerc's French troops after a stormy little battle in the Hôtel Meurice. Perhaps it was because of this news that at last you could really walk from L'Etoile to the Bastile wearing a tri-coloured rosette if you wished, and not be in imminent danger of finding yourself in the middle of a battle. Perhaps it was only the spontaneous combustion of history and humanity thrown together with great and sudden violence.

At any rate, Paris began about 9 A.M. to boil with the rushing color of a dye-maker's vat. Where one flag had been, there soon were two. Where there had been a newsboy, a tired *gendarme* or a two-man patrol of the F.F.I., there were now about a hundred men and five hundred women and children. Probably most of them, or at any rate some of them, left their homes with eminently practical errands in mind, but once they had begun to gravitate to the centre of the city, they became the prisoners of a surging rush of emotion, the like of which their city had not seen since the Revolution. Certainly they were as helpless to defend themselves against it as were the Parisians of 1789.

Everyone was on a bicycle and if ever I forget any of it I am sure the bicycles will be the last things I forget. If I said there were a million bicycles milling around the Place de l'Opéra this morning, it would be a highly unprofessional exaggeration, but if I had to make an estimate, I would still say there were a million bicycles.

And if I had to say how many beautiful brunette girls were riding bicycles, I could only say there were more beautiful brunettes than beautiful blondes. And if I had to say how many beautiful blondes there were, I could only say there were more beautiful blondes than beautiful redheads.

There was an unbelievably large number of all of them, and if I had to say how they were dressed I could only say that the women of Paris have the reputation of being the best-dressed in the world. That is one of the many things Hitler never quite managed to change.

The bicycles rolled up and down the boulevards in tens, in hundreds and in thousands. The morning became a sort of bloodless guerrilla war. You would drive your jeep slowly down one of the boulevards, and at an intersection you would suddenly be ambushed by two enfilading columns of bicycles and forced by sheer pressure of traffic to stop. At this point you were defeated.

59

The more agile Parisians would clamber to the hood, to the narrow dashboard, to the bumper of the jeep, and the more tender-hearted movie actresses would queue up for the privilege of kissing each of your sweaty unshaven cheeks.

Although it is of no interest to the general reading public, I must insert here, in the interests of my domestic future, a note to the effect that I managed to escape the worst horrors of this ordeal by sitting as aloofly as possible on the back seat and persuading a much better-suited conducting officer to work a double shift on the receiving line.

There was not much wine, but to superimpose wine on this sea of exhilaration would have been as clumsy as spiking champagne with corn whisky.

They began forming up early for the parade. The Maquis raced through the streets in long black cars and short brown cars, keeping their guns trained on the windows and roof tops, but even the Maquis, who really loved to fight, had not much fighting on their minds. The mass of people moved early toward the great avenue that stretches from L'Etoile to Notre-Dame, along the Champs Elysées through the Place de la Concorde and down the Rue de Rivoli. Flags and banners – *Vive de Gaulle, Vive la République, Vive les Alliés* – were waved along each bank of the thin channel the spectators could spare for those who were to be on parade.

All along the long route the swelling stream of humanity overflowed and filled all the road, sidewalk and boulevard space, spilled up into the avenue of plane trees along the Elysées, then spilled over again to the rooftops of the hotels and sidewalk cafés and the top of the Arc de Triomphe itself.

The Place de la Concorde was an acre of waving arms. We drove through it twice, once to get to L'Etoile before de Gaulle's arrival, and once to get back downtown after he had left. They were cheering everybody, of course, but because there were so few Canadians there, the cheers for Canada seemed louder than any others.

Riding this wild tide of acclaim on an Annie Oakley was a great experience, but it did seem wrong, if unavoidable, that of the Canadians that fought to make this day possible not one was there to see it, while a handful of newspapermen who did no fighting whatsoever took all the bows.

There were not many bands and not much ceremony. De Gaulle laid a wreath on the Tomb of the Unknown Soldier and then in a moment the towering music of *La Marseillaise* tumbled down the hill from L'Etoile to the Concorde. De Gaulle strode out in front and the parade half-followed him and then half-enveloped him like a golf gallery swinging out behind the champion.

They were all represented – the deputies from Algiers, the Invalide, the war veterans of 1914 and the veterans of 1940, the Red Cross, the Defense Passive, the Boy Scouts, the police, the F.F.I., the firemen and the postmen. None was cheered more joyously than the postmen; for it was anything but a solemn parade. Grinning soldiers of the Leclerc Division rode by waving from armoured cars.

All the marching groups started out hopefully and with brave resolutions. If the policemen marched as finely as the Grenadiers, the firemen marched even better. But before the head of the procession was half-way to the Concorde the whole project had broken down and the parade became less a parade than a promenade.

The idea seized a million people almost simultaneously that a formal procession was not what the occasion called for at all. It was an occasion that called for cheers and waves for the marchers, but if the marchers could not cheer and wave right back the whole enterprise would lose its flavor. And so after the first few hundred yards, Paris was cheering the parade and the parade was turning its head and grinning and losing step and waving and cheering Paris in return.

FRENCH VS. PATOIS

Somewhere in France (September 6, 1944)

To: The Berlitz School of Languages,
   321 Oxford Street,
   London, England.

Gentlemen:

I know you will be most eager to learn how I have been making out on the thirty-four lessons in French you were kind enough to sell me last April and May and, for my part, I am only too eager to tell you.

I have no reason to believe, gentlemen, that you spoke anything but the solemn truth when you assured me that an hour a day in the hands of your faculty would improve my French beyond recognition. If anything this was an understatement. I am in no way bitter about it, but I would like to suggest a slight moderation in your method of teaching. If I ever take another course from you – say, in Japanese or one of the Hindustani dialects in preparation for the next campaign – I would like you to attach a sort of guide or accent-watcher for me, keeping him constantly at my side and having him apply continuous and daily tests to my accent, like the man who is said to watch over the melons in the garden of the Shah of Persia. Then when I am ripe for plucking – that is to say, when my Japanese or Hindustani has improved within, but not beyond, recognition – then and precisely then, no sooner and no later, I would ask that the accent-watcher whisk me swiftly away to a dark room and keep me there, aloof from the world and free of all further academic influence, until I am ready to go into action. With the French course, it is obvious to me now that we should have stopped somewhere around the twenty-ninth lesson.

We carried the thing too far. We allowed our judgment to be dazzled, gentlemen, by the evanescent rainbow of perfection. One can carry perfection too far.

The factor we overlooked was a small one. I am prepared to share with you the responsibility for neglecting its perils. I remember clearly now the morning on which it was first drawn to my attention, and I know now what I should have done. Professor Beaudin, I think it was – the little bald man with the spectacles, anyway – Professor Beaudin said one day, *"Il faut con –"* never mind, gentlemen, I'll put it in English. Professor Beaudin said that it was necessary to remember that in many French provinces and districts the people do not speak the true French at all, but a local patois. In some sections, like parts of Brittany, this local patois has virtually no relation to the true French and the people do not even understand the true French. I can see now that instead of looking right on out the window at the buses I should have perked up at once and said: "Hold on, professor, let's get this straight."

If we had arrived at a firm understanding about this patois business right at the start and taken steps about it, I feel that a great many misunderstandings might have been nipped in the bud, or *tué dans l'oeuf*, if you prefer it that way. Instead of plunging into conversation with every Frenchman I met on the bald assumption that he spoke French, I should know enough to begin by asking directly, *"Parlez-vous patois?"* If the answer were in the affirmative, I should then stalk away and seek companionship and information elsewhere, thus sparing the poor wretch the embarrassment of having it dragged out of him by painful degrees that he did not even understand his own mother language.

When a person who speaks the pure French becomes inadvertently entangled in conversation with a person who speaks patois, and neither is aware of the other's infirmity, the results, I assure you, gentlemen, are sometimes enough to make a strong man tremble. On the way into Paris I stopped at a small restaurant on the roadside for a glass of wine. It did not occur to me that in a village so close to the capital they would speak anything but the distilled Parisian French, so I sailed right in, without fencing, and started to talk to the patroness, a kindly though rather severe and spinsterish woman of about sixty. Like everyone else on the road into Paris, it was ten to one that she had relatives in the city; it was an anxious time for all French people, and I wished to be particularly careful to impress upon this excellent woman that although we of the Allied armies could not share Paris's suffering, we could at least be sympathetic.

I chose what I consider a skilful and well-balanced opening. "Is there much hunger in Paris?" I inquired in my most anxious tones. You know far better than I do, gentlemen, that this translates as *"Ya-t-il beaucoup de faim à Paris?"*

The fatal word, gentlemen, was the word *"faim."* It seems that, in whatever patois this poor woman spoke the word *"faim"* is easily confused with *"femmes."* I thought the lady looked puzzled when she asked me to repeat the question, but, game to the core, I tried again, speaking more slowly and clearly to give her every chance. This time she looked shocked and even indignant. When she sniffed, in French, "Yes, Monsieur, I suppose you will find lots of women in Paris," I made a last babbling attempt to retrieve the situation. "I mean," I said, still in the true Parisian French, "Is there enough for the unfortunate people to eat?" The nuances here entirely escaped her, although I believe she understood that I was referring in some way to food, since I had taken the trouble to point meaningfully toward my mouth. Thereupon the untutored woman threw back her head and walked away. To her dying day she will be telling her neighbours, in patois: "Yes, yes, the Canadians are fine people. Their only interest in the liberation of Paris was to chase women and fill their bellies."

When I got to Paris, I discovered that, even there, there are minor patois into which the pure Parisian French divides. I had little difficulty in Paris, however, as I was in the almost constant company of a man who would permit me to listen to other people speaking French, but would scarcely permit me to speak a word myself. My companion was Sholto Watt, the correspondent of *The Montreal Star*.

Watt studied as a youth at the Sorbonne, and whatever patois it is they speak at the Sorbonne, he still speaks it with great fluency and grace, a circumstance which many Parisians commented on during our stay in the Ritz Hotel. Watt is a charming but in some ways a ruthless man. I am not yet certain why he would not allow me to exercise my Parisian French in its cradle and natural habitat; possibly it was to avoid the possibility of humiliating any of the many of his Parisian friends who called on us by exposing their inability to converse in anything but patois. At any rate Watt suppressed all my efforts to get off even the most elementary speech, with arbitrary finality.

The visitor would turn to me and say beamingly, *"Et parlez-vous français, Monsieur?"* Before I could assure him that I did, Watt would leap in, croaking, "Not one word," and then he would launch forth on such a torrent of his Sorbonne patois that I had no opportunity either to deny or disprove the inexplicable misstatement until the visitor was gone.

One afternoon I grew tired of this and determined, by fair means or foul, to give my Parisian French one brief airing before it was time to go. There inevitably came a lull in Watt's defensive monologue. I seized the visitor with a hypnotic stare and said, *"Pensez-vous, Monsieur—"*

A look of sheer horror crossed Watt's face. He looked wildly about the room like a haunted man. I saw a flash of cunning race across his mask of horror and he cried wildly, "The snipers again! Down! Here! On the floors! Silence, everybody, for your lives!"

Personally I couldn't hear a thing, and tried to say so. But our visitor was so rattled that he left anyway. I feel that I was tricked, but in this instance I wish to say that I do not hold the Berlitz School of Languages responsible in any way.

Yours faithfully,
RALPH ALLEN

With the Canadians in France (September 12, 1944)

This is going to be a hard point to get across without being misunderstood. Seeing the liberation of Paris made you admire Paris. Seeing the liberation of Brussels made you admire Brussels. And seeing both made you admire London more than you ever admired London before.

It is natural to compare these three capitals, whose destinies have been so closely intertwined through two wars. It is also dangerous, for if you try to make any orderly, clean-cut comparisons you inevitably will get into a hopeless argument with yourself.

How would you compare them? By saying there are meat and eggs and wine and even ice-cream in Brussels, perhaps? But then you would have to add that there is bread in London, and that there has always been enough bread for everyone. By saying there are still the world's most lavish gowns and most expensive perfumes to be bought in Paris, perhaps? But then you would have to say that in London you can still buy a meal of sorts for two and sixpence.

You can't pin down the effects of a war to its effects on the price of champagne any more than you can pin it down to location and acreage of a given area of destruction. And yet the same thought must have come to everyone who has seen Paris, Brussels and London within the last four months. Physically London has suffered far more than either of the others, and the sufferings of its people, although of a different kind, have not been less.

No one who did not live under the German occupation has the right to say how life in Brussels and Paris was between 1940 and 1944; for you cannot, after all, judge the sufferings a prisoner has undergone by weighing him at the end of his sentence. But those of us who lived in London between those years as rather privileged guests are only beginning to realize, after our first look into Europe, that life for the average Londoner was far harder than we or he quite knew. Life in London was dreary and sombre and chilling – a life whose tedium was relieved by its sudden dangers, until even the dangers become tedious too. Under German fire-bombs the Londoner saw his city in flames, and under high explosives he saw some of its oldest landmarks crumble. He

65

saw the blitz beaten and he saw the greater terror of the flying bomb return in its place.

If he had small children he sent them to the country, brought them back, and sent them away again. If his wife was young she went to work in a factory or an office. If the castle an Englishman calls his home was fortunate enough to escape the bombs, it still was only an empty shell. The food was skimpy and absurdly dull. A man could buy a suit of clothes a year, provided he didn't want to buy shirts or shoes. A woman could buy a dress if she didn't choose to buy stockings. The Londoner worked hard by day. Two nights a week he fire-watched or turned out with the Home Guard. For recreation there were the parks and shows, for which, like everything else, he had to queue up. And above everything and worse than almost anything there was the blackout, that great, relentless, inky paw that picked the whole city up each night – six o'clock on winter nights, ten o'clock on summer nights – and dropped it limp and lifeless and devoid of cheer into a bottomless abyss from which it would be reclaimed next morning. They watered the whisky and taxed it atrociously, and finally all but hounded it off the market. And in these last months a still more savage blow fell – the pubs began locking the doors behind signs that read: "Sorry, no beer today."

In Paris and in Brussels the *Gestapo* were shooting Frenchmen and Belgians. More than a million Frenchmen were prisoners of war in Germany, and several hundred thousand more were taken away as conscript labourers. Human life is no fit subject for entry in a logbook, but for every man or woman the *Gestapo* killed in Paris and Brussels, the *Luftwaffe* and the flying bombs must have killed or wounded four or five English men and women in London.

There was scarcely a London home that had not some close relative groping through the sand of Libya, the snow of the Apennines, or scrambling up the beaches of Normandy.

The one thing they had in London that they didn't have in Brussels or in Paris was freedom, and there can be no book entry on that. But even the freedom that London held was rudimentary and tenuous and hedged in by the maddening little slaveries of bureaucracy. The Englishman had spent a large part of the war years in forcing himself to obey regulations in which he had no real belief. In France and Belgium the regulations were made by the enemy, and French and Belgians at least had the luxury of disobeying them as often as they could. The greatest tribute to the Englishman's discipline was that, although there was a black market, it never attained the proportions of a major industry.

In fairness to the French and Belgians, it must be said that the gargantuan black markets that were established in both their countries were designed, at least partly, to frustrate German pillage. But the black markets of France and Belgium also kept the rich well fed and made many a small merchant rich. In England the small merchants grew poor and the rich, a large percentage of the rich at any rate, ate Woolton pie.

I do know that, having seen each of the other two cities on the first day of its freedom, I would like to see London on the day of the armistice. In its own way London's celebration will be no less memorable and gaudy than the others. The flags will come out, there will be dancing in Piccadilly Circus, and bonfires in Trafalgar Square. The now-obdurate pubkeepers will confess they've been hiding a few under the counter, after all. There will be much public kissing, indiscriminate but chaste. The women won't be so beautiful as the women of Paris, partly because they weren't so beautiful in the first place, and partly because they have been too busy collecting tickets on buses or turning lathes in factories to worry much about catching up. Some of them will be wearing cosmetics – but not all of them, because there's not enough lipstick and powder to go around. Some of them will be wearing new dresses, but most of them will be wearing neatly pressed tweed suits and flat shoes.

I don't think that even on armistice night the people of London will be hard to recognize. The chances are along toward morning the taxi-drivers, if you can find them, will be starting to snarl at their fares and the bobbies will be saying politely but firmly, "Come along now, please," and the waitress at Lyons all-night corner-house will be suggesting helpfully, "Like to try the spam and mashed, dearie? It's really not bad."

The party will break up in time for an astonishing part of London to get back to work the next morning, steadfast and disciplined and complaining as a soldier complains, for complaining's own sake. This is as London has been throughout. And in Paris and Brussels they will be the first to tell you that if London had been different there would have been no parade this year in the Champs Elysées, and no dancing in the Place Bouckère.

With the Canadian First Army in France (September 13, 1944)

For all its horror the war has yielded its days of magic.

The Americans found theirs on the high road from Brittany to Paris; the British theirs on the dash through a half-mad Brussels.

But for the Canadians there are still only the smoking hills of Boulogne-sur-Mer and the soggy trenches of the Belgian lowlands.

It has become a rough war again in every sector as the Germans make use of every extra hour that our extended supply lines have given them to dig in frantically behind the Siegfried Line and the Albert Canal.

Over here it has never really been anything else. That doesn't mean the Canadians have had to fight harder than anybody else. It only means that through conditions of geography and strategy – both our own strategy and the enemy's – our troopers have had a more meagre allotment of the days of magic, those rarefied and heady days when the guns grow silent, the flags break out on row after row of unscarred buildings and the grimiest tank-driver or the greasiest corporal cook can ride down a magic boulevard and feel like a knight errant riding down the field of the cloth of gold.

Among the days like that were August 25, 26 and 27 in Paris; and September 3, and 4, and, in fact, all last week in Brussels. There was one such day for the Canadian 2nd Division in Dieppe.

But geography and strategy so far have decreed that for the Canadians there should be no others.

The geography was simple enough. There simply wasn't any Paris or Brussels in our line of march. The strategy was simple, too. The Germans simply decided in the first ecstatic phase of the Western Front that nothing was so important to them as holding the right flank of their line in the vicinity of Caen and Falaise, and in the second or mobile phase they decided that nothing was so important as to deny us the use of the major Channel ports.

And so from June 6 to August 16 Canadian troops were fighting through a twenty-five mile-long strip of virtually uninhabitable rubble.

Some of the rubble was there before they came, a terrible

legacy of the terrible power of the Allied air forces. Some of it the soldiers had to make themselves.

The small percentage of the people of Caen who had remained in the small percentage of homes that stood through the bombardment came out to give them a kingly welcome when they passed through the city at last. But however a soldier could feel in the streets of Caen it could not be like a king.

There was too much tragedy in the wrecked houses that still smouldered and in the eyes that were still troubled as they smiled. The soldiers passed through with troubled eyes and found the Germans already waiting across the river in the suburbs.

There were five weeks more of making rubble, of killing Germans and being killed, and then Falaise fell. It was another Caen.

The Falaise Gap was different and it was also far better than anything the Canadians had experienced before. The chase surged through the reeking corridor and then spilled on to the green, open country beyond.

But though it rolled in headlong triumph now, after ten livid, bitter, deathly weeks, the 1st Canadian Army still rolled down no trim and smiling boulevards.

The next big town was Lisieux, and the next Rouen. At Lisieux nothing stood but a convent, a cathedral and a few houses. To block the German reinforcements on the road to D-Day beaches, the air force had already levelled the city.

Rouen, a strategical target first, and then a tactical target because it commanded so many of the vital Seine bridges, left another memory of wounds.

In the quick dash from the Seine to Belgium the almost unrelieved view of tragedy which the Canadian soldiers had been seeing in Northern Europe lifted for a few days. And then it dropped again.

All the cities lay on the left flank, that is, on the Channel coast. For a day or two it was uncertain how tenaciously the Germans would defend them. Now it has become apparent that, except for Dieppe and Ostend, the Germans have determined to defend them all at any cost.

If the Germans persist in squandering whole cities and the lives of noncombatants alike for the sake of a few days or weeks, then it seems almost inevitable that the dual tragedy of Le Havre will be repeated at Boulogne, Dunkirk and Calais.

And if the Germans decree it must be so when Canadian soldiers go into Calais, Dunkirk and Boulogne, the things they see will be much the same things they have seen all along the way.

Perhaps if you must see a war and particularly if you must fight it, it is better to see it this way. Perhaps it is better not to get even one day of war mixed up with bands and cheers and flowers.

And yet as the troops of the 1st Canadian Army sit in the hills of Boulogne and in the soggy trenches of the Northern lowlands it is hard not to wish that every man who sits there waiting couldn't have been in Paris on August 26 or in Brussels on September 4.

WHY DON'T THE HUNS SURRENDER?

With the First Canadian Army in Germany (March 5, 1945)

Even the infantry, the war's firmest realists, are beginning to join in the cry of the civilians – "Why don't the Germans quit?" From London to Calcar this is the Western Front's hottest question. It will never be answered to anyone's satisfaction until we learn to reject the sweet nothings of our own propaganda and revise our thinking about the Germans as drastically as they have sometimes made us revise our battle plans.

There should be no mystery in the Germans' continued resistance. But the "mystery" persists because we persevere, almost to the exclusion of reason, in ignoring the unpleasant fact that the Germans have some characteristics in common with the rest of the human race. For thirty-one years we have tried to explain everything the Germans have done by their dissimilarities from ourselves. Now we are at a loss to explain what they are doing because they are doing it, not under the complusion of their dissimilarities, but under the compulsion of certain pronounced and demonstrable likenesses.

The Germans have courage, they love their country and their homes, and they have an appetite for causes. This is not the pronouncement of an expert, but a conclusion based on the observation of thousands of Germans. It is these characteristics which keep the Germans fighting now. The other compulsions are not yet dead – the urge for self-aggrandizement, the nation-persecution complex, the blind faith in Hitler, the fear of Himmler – but they have become secondary.

German resistance today is mainly founded on something much less and if we continue to assess it only in the light of shibboleths we will remain up against a wall of incomprehension. Until we can bring ourselves to realize that unconditional surrender means to the German of today exactly what the spectre of Brownshirts in Whitehall meant to the Englishman in 1940, we will have as much trouble rationalizing the Germans' acceptance of Allied bombing as they had in rationalizing the British acceptance of the blitz. Until we discard the false parallel of 1918 – when the German home front was less highly disciplined and half of ravaged Europe was not pressing in on the Reich for revenge – our confusion will be only deepened.

Nowhere have Allied appraisals of the German's capacity for resistance erred more consistently than in the tents, caravan trucks and impromptu offices of our intelligence staff officers. From D-Day on the chronically pessimistic statements of German prisoners of war and the chronically optimistic conclusions of our intelligence branch have been neatly dovetailed into a picture of German morale which had it only been half true at any time would have ensured peace long before Christmas.

Our Intelligence is not inaccurate, it simply refuses to face reality. Nor was its hair-raising fatuity visibly shaken by the Ardennes offensive. Before Rundstedt's push was three days old correspondents were hearing that the German drive "would really shorten the war." For nine months we have been strongly inclined to interpret our smallest scraps of information about the enemy to conform with the preconceived belief that the Germans cannot absorb reverses.

As early as D-Day plus four an Intelligence officer told me in Normandy: "The Germans are in desperate shape already. They're using artillerymen as infantry." His facts were right, but he drew his conclusions with a long, long bow.

Today I asked an interrogation officer at a prisoner-of-war cage what he had been hearing lately.

"A German officer just came down the line, saw our stuff rolling up and said: 'If the German High Command knew how powerful you were the war would be over already.' There was another officer who said: 'I felt it was compatible with my honour to surrender today because the entire Wehrmacht is going to surrender tomorrow.' And the other day I heard about one of our recce patrols that got lost in a German town and was hidden by German civilians until we took the town over."

"What does it add up to?" I asked.

"Nothing, probably," the interrogation officer said. "We've been getting people like that in dribs and drabs all the time. But by the time the information gets back to the army or army group I suppose they will decide it means another crack in enemy morale."

There are still at least sixty-five million Germans inside the dwindling borders of the Reich – most of them healthy, well fed and efficiently integrated into a war machine which, however battered, is not yet broken. If it is not clear to us what alternatives they see to total defeat, we can surely remember in our groping for logic that it was not clear to the world what alternatives Britain had in 1940 or Russia in 1941.

If there is an answer to the question, "Why don't the Germans quit?" it is the simplest answer. They are not yet finally beaten.

DECEPTIVE SPRING

On the Western Front (March 21, 1945)

Spring came to Europe today like a streetwalker's smile, full of fradulent allure, half-hidden tragedy and high promise at a cost. On the season's first day it was a spring of shattering contrasts – of fashion showings in Paris and of grey hunger in Alsace; of reopening sidewalk cafes jammed with soldiers in Brussels and of ambulance convoys moving slowly across the pontoon bridge at Remagen; of spring seeding in the distant fields of Normandy and of Dutch school-children stopping their play to watch the robot bombs race down toward Antwerp; of crocuses and budding tulips writing life from between the dead, wet shell-scars of the Northern front; of pine-wood air fouled by the sour cadavers of little German cities.

Of blue skies filled with the throbbing menace of bombers. Of sleek men who never lost their sleekness driving good cars on the roads of France and Belgium and lean grey women who will never lose their leanness lining up for bread. Of German men dying wretchedly for the Reich under the arm of the Moselle while the fathers and mothers who dedicated them to this end shuffle woodenly into refugee camps muttering wooden curses against the things they taught their sons to die for.

It was a spring of burning shadows, and enveloping it all was the noisy impatient rustle of history, pouring men and arms into the bloodstained craw of the Rhine. For the first time the front-line in spring offered Europe a demonstrable hope of peace. To most of the Europeans who live on this side of the Rhine, the peace has already begun. To the visiting soldiers waiting on the Rhine to pick up the check it is not that simple, but for once the men who have to do the fighting have almost persuaded themselves to go along with the chronic optimism of men who don't. For the first time the front-line infantryman has substantially the same views about the end of the war as the staff officer in the back areas and the civilian patron of the BBC.

Three months ago if you asked an infantryman about the end of the European war he was apt to say, "If you know some new way to stop them bloody mortars coming over we can finish it next Tuesday. If not, let's quit kidding." Now the same soldier is apt to say, "June, maybe." There are a few soldiers who think it will end as early as April, and a few who think it may even stretch into fall.

But June is the month that leads all the polls. Most of those who guess June will bring peace work from the same rough logic – a month to cross the Rhine, a month to regroup and build up, another month to make it stick – always, of course, with the help of Uncle Joe.

Peace and the Rhine are not the sole occupants of the soldier's thoughts on this first day of spring. The classic cliché of war correspondents, "Our boys are eager for another crack at Jerry," has never had much basis of truth, and it was never less true than today. Any normal man who has been through one battle doesn't look forward to the next, no matter how unshaken his nerves and ideals may be, and no matter how severely his neglect to do so may deny the traditional concepts.

Most of the men waiting beside the Rhine find other things to think about. The Americans talk about the Far East, or the New York curfew, and make affectionate jokes about the Russians and guilty jokes about the fraternization ban, which is slightly more successful than the ban on gambling in Toronto.

The British talk about Beveridge, and in disturbed voices about the capacity of their country to raise the standard of living. The Canadians talk about the home leave scheme, about the Zombies (fairly politely), about Burma, about the blueprints for rehabilitation which most of them recognize as a genuine sign of their country's desire to do well by them when they get home.

73

Today's correspondence column of *Maple Leaf* was completely absorbed by letters about the 1936 Canadian Olympic hockey team, whose picture the paper had run earlier with a request for identification.

Yesterday's correspondence was headed by a sergeant's question whether it was true that N.R.M.A. draftees were being allowed to wear the Canadian volunteer ribbon (the paper answered no), and by a witty and good-natured bachelor's beef against the home-leave regulation which gives married men an edge over single men.

A person who could only stop to exchange the time of day would not find much change in the thinking of our army between last spring and this. A great constitutional change has occurred nevertheless. Our army has grown cynical – some would say healthily – of the security of the peace toward which it has given so many of its years and so much of its blood.

Whether it was naïveté or faith, most of our soldiers came to Normandy firmly believing that by helping to defeat Germany they could guarantee peace for the rest of their lives and perhaps for the lives of their children.

They haven't had much time to look at the panorama of Europe boiling into shape in the wake of their trudging footsteps, but much of what they have seen has raised half-spoken doubts and half-named fears. Perhaps they have seen it only in the clip-joints of Paris and the black markets of Brussels, but they have all seen greed at work openly and even flamboyantly, above apology and free of shame.

They have seen the first clutching for power over the still-warm bodies of Europe's greatest heroes, the men of the underground. They have seen shrill and murderous squabbles between one group which would use the dead heroes for political currency and another group which would deny them even the honour they earned at the grave. The blindest of them have seen that whatever the dwellers in the temperate zone of Europe have learned, all of the extreme reactionaries and most of the extreme leftists have refused to learn that they must get along together somehow.

It is too early to say that the average Canadian soldier has lost confidence in the durability of the peace, but he has definitely lost confidence that it will come as an automatic reward like his gratuity cheque.

The last three officers I talked to about the peace made the same remark in different words. Paraphrased it was, "I'm going to stay in the reserve army after the war. I don't like soldiering and I figure I've paid my share of the shot for patriotism. But when I go next time I want to go with the high-priced help."

The lull on the lower Rhine has given its khaki-clad inhabitants a chance for more pleasant preoccupations. A few of them have been getting to Brussels on 48-hour leaves. Practically all of them are catching up on their laundry, their mail and their baths.

Movies are running overtime and the forward areas are rampant with troupes of British E.N.S.A. entertainers, practically all of whom try stubbornly to be funny in the face of a general batting-average that would discourage the scorekeeper for the Phillies. The Rhine is never far away, mocking the unnatural tranquility spring has brought to our part of the front and daring it to last. It will be the last spring anyway. Everybody knows that now.

Even the Rhine can't take that away from them.

TREK TO THE RHINE

Beinen, Germany (March 28, 1945)

The death throes of this little Rhineland town were over today. The shelling eased up some time in the night and when the fog cleared on a sunless morning, the hundred civilians who had toughed out a tough battle in their sturdy cellars came up to see whether it was worthwhile trying to live here any more. All they saw was a bed of jagged stalagmites rising above an acre of fresh rubble. The only whole thing in the place was the base of the Beinen war memorial to the dead of 1914-18, and the Prussian eagle which surmounted it had had a wing torn off. Just below it lay a dead German of this war with his right leg blown up under his armpit.

Before any one had a chance to give them orders, the people of Beinen started evacuating toward the Rhine.

They packed up what they could carry on their backs or push in baby carriages, wheelbarrows or handcarts, and headed for the south-west in a ragged convoy that weaved across the clammy green fields for more than two miles. At first they stuck to the road but when the military traffiic moving up grew thicker they veered off to the soggy tank tracks, zigzagging to miss the tallest bumps and the new slit trenches that strewed the ground.

Even for refugees, they moved slowly. As refugees always do, they were trying to carry far bigger loads than were practical, and unlike most columns of refugees this one had no men to handle its heaviest bundles. In Italy, France, Belguim and Holland there were always a few sturdy men mixed up with the women and children, and even on the west bank of the River Rhine there were usually a few teen-aged boys to supply a little extra heart and help.

The few males who had been left behind here by the receding dragnet of the Wehrmacht were either so suspiciously young and healthy that they had been sent back to the prisoner-of-war camps for investigation, or so old and feeble that they were barely able to look after themselves.

One old man in a neat black serge suit struggled along near the head of the procession, pushing a wheelbarrow weighted down with suitcases. "All for Hitler," he cried sardonically as he put down his load.

A mile further down the column the gaunt, grey proprietor of a pushcart stopped when he saw us staring curiously at his unfamiliar uniform, deep blue pants and jacket with grey piping and a round peaked cap. He fumbled in his pocket and pulled out a piece of paper on which he had scrawled the crude drawing of a train.

"Railway," he said. Then he turned over his right hand and showed us a red dripping gash and asked if we could loan him a bandage. We told him he'd find a dressing-station just down the road. I asked him if he was a member of the Nazi Party. *"Ja,"* he said. He lifted his bloody hand in a mocking parody of the party salute, croaked *"Heil Hitler."*

These were almost the only men we saw, except for one very old and very detached gentleman who sat with his eyes screwed shut under several layers of pots and pans, and mattresses in a wheelbarrow. Two stout red-faced women who were propelling him had apparently loaded their ancient passenger first and then piled their household goods on top of him until there wasn't room for any more. Until I saw the old man turn his head, I thought he might be dead. After that, the only logical explanation for his firmly closed eyes seemed to be that he knew he wouldn't be seeing Beinen again, and he preferred to remember it some other way.

In another wheelbarrow, an old woman sat with two small girls between her legs while a slightly larger girl tugged in the front on a ready-made rope harness and a big woman shoved on the handles. Another family group was led by two little girls of perhaps six and seven each dressed in a peaked fur-fringed little hood and a plaid coat and struggling a few yards at a time with a big suitcase. Behind them two women pulled a cart, fairly overflowing with smoked hams, preserves, cooking utensils and bedding. From the rear of the cart were suspended two live chickens tucked into small white sacks.

A little further back a pretty girl tugged a small grey puppy. Every family seemed to have enough food to last three or four days at least, and some were already beginning to drop out and cook their first meal on the road beside an only partially damaged barn.

This was only part of the evacuation of the town of Beinen, and not the saddest part. As the refugees crawled on toward the bridges, they passed a long line of fresh excavations in the lee of an inland dike. This was to be the burial ground for more than forty Canadian soldiers who had died at the town approaches. They lay now beneath their grey blankets under the grey sky. One of them near the middle was wrapped in the Union Jack. He had been one of the best-beloved officers in his division and his whole battalion was to march up the road a little later to attend his burial.

The fighting at Beinen, along with that further down the road at Rees, probably presented the hardest fighting that Allied troops have met anywhere east of the Rhine. On the green flats outside it I think I saw more hastily dug trenches and more dead cattle than I had seen in a comparable area since before the breakthrough at Caen in Normandy.

We pushed through a naked orchard and over a mound of rubble into a cellar just in time to catch the colonel of the Highland Light Infantry climbing out of bed. The bed was a mattress beside a ceiling-high mound of turnips, and as the colonel sat up for his morning stretch he said, "This is the best night's sleep I've had in three months."

The colonel talked for a while about the fighting. On the way out a raffish medley of piano music in four-four time floated across the barnyard from a half-gutted machine-shed. Private Mike Medwick of Kitchener, Ontario, exhausted his limited repertoire and closed the dusty music-box.

I asked if he had been at Buron, thinking about the day his battalion took more than three hundred casualties going for a town that looked much like this one across much the same kind of country.

"I was there all right," he said. "Nothing has been quite like that, and we got seven or eight pretty soft days afterward. This Rhine stuff has been steady and mean. It's easing off now, but it has been pretty rough."

GOTTERDAMMERUNG

Aschendorf, Germany (April 24, 1945)

Another small corner of the world of Nazi Germany died here the other day. It was not a pretty or heroic death. As *Gotterdammerung* closed in, two thousand soldiers of the Wehrmacht – some good soldiers, some bad – descended to the common level of trapped animals. The strong murdered the weak in cold blood. The weak ratted on the helpless and in the last livid hour the voice of Hitler's Reich shrieked unheard in the crescendo of a slaughter pen.

The setting for the gory drama was a Wehrmacht prison camp two miles north from this German town. Its inhabitants were one hundred guards and three thousand soldiers serving sentences from a year to life for crimes ranging in degree from stealing from the wrong people to questioning the military genius of the Fuehrer. About one prisoner in three was a conscript or volunteer from occupied Europe. The rest were native Germans, many of them still Nazi in sympathies despite their fall from grace.

It was three weeks ago, according to the testimony of the few prisoners who are still living among the camp's smoking ruins, that the sense of impending doom first began to overtake the place. They got little news in the prisoners' compound but they knew vaguely that the war was going very badly. One day the inmates were lined up in the compound and told that they were to be given a "talk" by a paratroop officer.

When the officer began to speak the lines of prisoners remained rigid and unmoving, but a current of dread ran through the ranks. The man wore the uniform of a paratrooper, but he talked like an ss man – shouting, denouncing, cursing, threatening, his lips and face white with fury.

"In Germany now, wherever the ss goes, it leaves the mark of death," one of the prisoners said today. "They work through fear and hate, but the fear and hate of the ss is now so great that it merely turns men to jelly. But anyone who has offended the laws of the leaders knows only too well how to recognize the ss without the help of his badges."

The visiting officer harangued the prisoners for an hour. Even this audience, long experienced in the technique of Nazi indoctrination, could only guess what he was getting at. He called them cowards, traitors, assassins of the Fatherland. Then he walked down the ranks, stopping here and there to call a man out. "Why are you here?" he would scream. "I robbed a citizen of Germany, Herr Hauptmann."

"You deserve to be shot, don't you?" *"Ja wohl, Herr Hauptmann."*

"Why are you here?" "I spoke disloyally of our Fuehrer."

"You deserve to be shot, don't you?" *"Ja wohl, Herr Hauptmann."*

The parade was dismissed. For a week and a half the uneasy inmates of the camp were allowed to build unnamed fears, fearful hopes, and then to tear them down again. The suspense mounted daily and with it the flood of rumours, some encouraged by the guards one day and scoffed at the next. The only certain thing was that the Hauptmann had not been talking for the exercise. Something momentous was coming. The camp's personnel had become a burden on the Reich.

All but the most trivial offenders were to be executed. No, the Wehrmacht had chosen to arm the camp and send it against the Allies on a suicide mission. It was neither of those. The inmates were to be released and allowed to volunteer for service in the army or to find their way back to their homes.

"But still, as we whispered at our toil in the camp workrooms, we felt the mark of death," said the prisoner.

Men still died each day from hunger and disease, but that was only routine. Suspicion and conspiracy took possession of the camp as the tension grew. In the night a man would whisper to his bunk-mate, "Germany is defeated. It is Hitler's doing." His comrade would say nothing, but in the morning there would be another summary trial in the commandant's office. In the afternoon another execution, and at night another man flung lonely in the darkness, wondering what his reward would be for the betrayal of his friend. The hut leaders, whose power was more absolute than the power of the guards, began to practice extortion openly, not even troubling to name the penalties for non-submission.

As edged nerves began to crack, a few men made the hopeless attempt to scale the three high barriers of barbed wire and escape across the surrounding peat-moors. They were escorted into the dark building marked "arrest" and shot without trial.

At least eleven days ago there was another parade. This time it was the camp commandant, a boy of twenty-three, who spoke to the men. He repeated the threats and curses of the SS captain and then said, "All men who are spiritually fit to serve the Fatherland will be allowed to join the Volkssturm. They will receive training here and will be sent into action when the time is ripe."

It was good news for the "spiritually fit." For the unfit it was the end. The same afternoon one hundred and sixty prisoners whose offense had been desertion from the Wehrmacht were assembled at the end of the compound and divided into groups of five.

A light anti-aircraft gun on a mobile mounting was brought into the compound. In succession the young commandant gave the same order to each group of live men: "About turn." Without emotion or any sign of will, each group obeyed, turning swiftly to face the wire. The big slugs ripped into their backs and the gun rolled on down the line until its work was done.

The training of the new recruits in the Volkssturm began. But on the very first day a new and still more ominous threat fell like a grey shadow across the camp. Gunfire echoed in the distance, and a German anti-aircraft battery took up gun positions in the woods adjoining the camp. Allied Typhoons began ranging overhead. Conscious of their helplessness and vulnerability, the prisoners looked through the wire with mounting fear and swore apprehensively each time they saw flame spurt from the German gun positions. Twice the Typhoons found the guns. Twice the guns moved, each time closer to the camp.

The camp was by now in a state of thinly suppressed panic, yet the commandant made no move to open the prison gates. The inmates spent all their spare time digging slit trenches between the huts and the stone work-houses. Their longing eyes turned with envy and helpless anger to the big concrete shelter in the guards' compound a few yards away from the last strand of wire.

Finally the probing Typhoons blasted out the last wood and drove the guns out on the open plain. Their sweating, fearful crews dug them in and did what they could to provide camouflage against the boundaries of the camp itself.

There was one more day of reprieve. The commandant allowed three hundred of the "best" prisoners to move into the guards' compound before being sent to the Volkssturm.

Then, one morning early this week, the Typhoons found the German guns again.

Their first roaring swoop threw the camp into an awful pandemonium and salvos of rockets raked back and forth in a straight line from gun site to gun site. The camp was in flames in a matter of moments. As the swishing rockets tore through the soft shoulders of their trenches and brought the burning huts around them in a red torrent, the helpless prisoners rushed to the wire leading to the big shelter in the guards' compound and screamed for mercy. Hundreds of them tried to claw their way through the wire.

Between strikes by the Typhoons the commandant gave his answer. He brought a machine-gun to the top of the shelter and cut the prisoners down like rabbits. A few of them broke through and ten guards were killed in the hand-to-hand battle that followed beneath the thudding hail of British rockets.

The planes destroyed the guns outside and left the prison camp a burning billiard-table. As soon as the attack ended the commandant fled with the guards and his three hundred privileged Volkssturm candidates. How many prisoners were killed by Typhoons and how many by the Germans it is impossible to guess. When the Polish armoured division captured the camp the day after the Typhoons hit it, there were fewer than a hundred men still there and still able to walk. Today in their loose-fitting prisoners' costumes of black and yellow cotton they moved through the smouldering wreckage like gaunt and dingy harlequins, burying all they could find of five hundred corpses.

The years immediately after the war were for Ralph Allen, as for so many others of his generation, an unsettled time. He went back briefly to *The Globe and Mail,* published a war novel called *Homemade Banners,* and then in 1946 joined the staff of *Maclean's Magazine* as an assistant editor.

The man who hired him was W. Arthur Irwin, then editor of *Maclean's,* later a Canadian Ambassador and publisher of the *Victoria Daily Times.* Irwin recognized that Allen had the makings of an editor and kept "pushing at him, as quickly as he could take them on, the various duties connected with editing a magazine."

During this whole post-war period, Ralph could not make up his mind whether he wanted, as Irwin put it, "to be the conductor of the orchestra or the first violin" and the conflict between his desire to write and the demands his conscience and pocketbook made that he should put to use his talent for editing was to plague him until he died. "There isn't any doubt in my mind that what Ralph wanted was to be a full-time writer, a novelist," Birdeen Allen remarked after his death, "but he had a family to support and he didn't want us to go through the kind of financial hardship he'd experienced as a child."

In 1949, he gave up his position as managing editor of *Maclean's* to write a sports column for the Toronto *Telegram,* a job he thought he could cope with easily during the day-time and still have enough creative energy left over to write novels at night.

He soon found he had lost his taste for writing sports. (He told Trent Frayne at the time that the trouble with the job was "you have to go to all those goddam games".) Later that year, when Irwin left *Maclean's,* he was easily able to persuade the publishers that Ralph was the natural choice as his successor and with the first issue in February, 1950, Ralph Allen became the magazine's fifth editor.

Maclean's had a worthy, if not greatly distinguished history. It had been started in 1905 (as *The Busy Man's Magazine*) by the founder of the Maclean-Hunter publishing empire, Colonel John Bayne Maclean, a tough old patriot with Imperialist leanings, who wanted (as Ralph Allen described it in a tribute to Maclean when he died) "to give Canada a national voice . . . at a time when there were no Canadian periodicals speaking to a general audience of Canadians on Canadian terms."

The magazine had tottered uncertainly toward the realization of this goal until Arthur Irwin took hold of it in the early forties, after twenty years of working there as a sub-editor. Irwin supported the Colonel's vision but he was a patriot of a different order, one of the first of the new nationalists who saw Canada's future as lying outside the influence of Great Britain, as a bicultural nation with an independent stature and an independent voice.

Ralph came strongly under Irwin's influence, and quoted him often on this point and others, but he brought to the editor's chair his own concept of Canadian nationalism and his own ideas about how to run a magazine.

"We were nationalists, too," said Pierre Berton, who had been hired by Irwin and was first Ralph Allen's articles editor and then his managing editor. "But we were as much in opposition to creeping Americanism as we were to the idea of the Empire, which was then a faded force. None of us knew much about magazines but we learned as we went along. We had it in our minds that we could beat on our own ground the American magazines that were being dumped across the border and give Canadians an in-depth look at their country they couldn't get anywhere else."

To achieve that objective, the new editors of *Maclean's* set about moulding a generation of magazine journalists by, as Berton described it, "starting a school of writing with Ralph Allen as the faculty."

Maclean's never did have any formal manual outlining its writing style. There was a printed memo called *"Maclean's* article requirements." All that is remembered of that old sheet is that it said, curiously and quite unnecessarily, *"Maclean's* eschews the gee-whiz style."

It did not take long for the high standards of reporting and writing set by the editor to cause the magazine "to be regarded by the extensive circle of its admirers within the profession with nervous awe" as June Callwood, a writer who was one of *Maclean's* most prolific and admired freelancers, described it.

Very few usable articles ever came into the magazine over the transom. Most of the ideas for articles originated from staff memos or brainstorming sessions, held first in the editor's office and later at editorial luncheons. These ideas were then assigned to staff writers or a select group of freelancers (a group that other writers bitterly – and not unjustifiably – complained it was almost impossible to join), researched extensively, often for as long as a month or more, written and submitted to the articles editor who would comment at length on the manuscript and then pass it "up the line" to Berton and Allen. ("Where's my piece?" writers would be heard asking, neurotically. "Up the line," secretaries would answer.)

The article would then, more often than not, come back to the writer to be re-written. Three re-writes were not uncommon; one staff writer later claimed his first article was done eleven times; and it was sufficiently remarkable when Barbara Moon wrote a profile of Nathan Cohen, the drama critic, that required only one word change, for the other writers to buy her champagne.

Once it had met the editor's approval, the story was sent on to the copy department to be titled, copy-edited and then checked by young college graduates in cashmere sweaters who looked on themselves and their duties with serious, superior eyes. The checking system was based roughly on what was known of the *New Yorker* method and many a writer cursed when he was told that par on a golf course in South Carolina was one stroke less than he had written or that the number of sacred cows in India was a hundred thousand more than he claimed. (One girl was renowned in this small circle, for sending out a checker's letter – under the usual imperious statement that these facts, unless challenged, would appear in an upcoming *Maclean's* – addressed to a man called something like Nicholas Papaladopolous and containing two facts: "1. You are a Greek *restauranteur*" and "2. You are the owner of Nick's Grill.")

The *Maclean's* staff took neither meekly nor joyfully to this rigorous regime. There were many complaints muttered furiously in writers' offices about the editors' unfeeling intransigence. (Significantly, the blame was usually placed not on Ralph's head but more broadly on "them", the "three wise men", the human links in that inhuman "line".)

Allen tempered his hard demands with meaningful praise; he gave his staff the confidence that can be inspired only by an editor who knows exactly what he wants and is capable himself of producing it; and his employees had a respect for their craft, their magazine and their colleagues that most of them had never known before and were unlikely to know again.

Ralph Allen was quick to point out after he left *Maclean's* the importance of the fact that while he edited it, he had the support of an enlightened publisher. Floyd Chalmers, who was vice-president and then president of Maclean-Hunter during Allen's tenure, was a man of intelligence and imagination who had been an editor himself (of the *Financial Post*), and had the great good sense not to interfere with the way an editor he had chosen and trusted ran his magazine.

The way Ralph Allen ran *Maclean's* during the fifties brought it close to the shimmering ideal he had set for himself. He commissioned articles, paintings, and photographs that probed into every corner of Canadian life; he published the essays of Canadian novelists and intellectuals (Hugh MacLennan, Arthur M. Lower, Morley Callaghan); he established the *Maclean's* novel award and the *Maclean's* short story contests; he introduced new features – the "Flashback" articles that brought Canadian history to life, the yellow pages first called "Preview" and then "Maclean's Reports" meant to bring more "hard news" to the magazine and the "For The Sake of Argument" column, which was later much copied by American publications.

More important than any of this, he succeeded in his ambition to put out a fairly and honestly edited magazine, that respected its readers' intelligence sufficiently to give them both sides of issues and then allow them to draw their own conclusions. (It was this very honesty that led *Maclean's* detractors to say that the magazine was lugubrious, that its emphasis on "balance" – one of Allen's favourite words – made it colourless. This was a charge to which its admirers, perhaps arrogantly, paid no heed.)

When Ralph Allen decided in the spring of 1960 to quit the magazine, to write his own books and contribute articles on a part-time basis, he said in response to the buzzing in the trade that there had been "no dust-up between *Maclean's* and me. I just want to get out from behind a desk for a while." But his friends continued to think there was more to his decision than he was willing to say and that his disenchantment with his job had begun two years earlier, in 1958.

His close friend and the longtime overseas correspondent for *Maclean's,* Lionel Shapiro, died of cancer in the spring of that year. Then in the late summer, Pierre Berton, who was Allen's mainstay, a dynamo of energy and an unfailing source of enthusiasm and ideas, left the magazine after a quarrel with the Maclean-Hunter management that resulted from a directive most sensible people, even at the time, thought was strange. (It insisted that no Maclean-Hunter editor could appear on a television program sponsored by a company that did not advertise in Maclean-Hunter magazines.) At the same time, *Maclean's* (and most other Canadian magazines) began to suffer from advertising losses as a result of the blooming of television, and the inroads made by the so-called "Canadian" editions of *Time* and *Readers' Digest.* Management began to show the nervousness that businessmen, viewing decreased profits, generally display.

In any case, Ralph Allen left *Maclean's* to the regret of the staff and – to be fair – of the publishers. He was succeeded, first by Blair Fraser, the magazine's Ottawa editor, who reluctantly agreed to take the job for two years, and then by Ken Lefolii, a writer in his early thirties, who drew around him a group of young editors and writers that Ralph Allen affectionately called "the Young Turks" and others, less affectionately named "the whiz kids." The magazine's publishers grew even more nervous in the next two years and soon ousted Lefolii, replacing him and seven members of his staff (who protested his dismissal by resigning in a body) with more predictable men. *Maclean's* later became a monthly, less concerned with leading Canadian opinion, more imitative of the big American leisure magazines.

Still, there isn't any doubt that to the journalists who preceded Ralph Allen, who worked with him and who succeeded him on the staff of *Maclean's,* the period of his editorship was the magazine's most successful era. Just why this was so is demonstrated, in part at least, by the editorials and articles that follow. They represent only a small fraction of the material Ralph Allen published in *Maclean's* and were chosen both because they illustrate his ideas and the style he formulated, and because they have the enduring quality of excellence which he optimistically (and often vainly) sought to insure would be characteristic of every piece of copy published in his magazine.

WAR IS HELL

(June 15, 1950)

"My tale is of war and hard work and enterprises, sometimes stirring but more often ludicrous; of sudden reversals of fortune . . . of bloodshed and violence, but more often of cunning and deceit and high spirits and the pleasant cudgeling of brains and then again more work; above all of friendship.

Only to the fools of my generation will the realization come as a surprise that we liked war."

These are not the words of a Roman centurion swash-buckling home from one of those cleanly exhilarating and slightly bush-league wars that poets used to write about. They're the words of an amateur soldier of the British Army and they apply to the latest and cruelest of all wars. The author is Vladimir Peniakoff and under the world-famous *nom de guerre* of Colonel Popski he has endured far more than his share of danger, pain and hardship and won far more than his share of distinction.

Colonel Popski is against war of course. Against the idea of war and against the people who start wars. In time of war he feels a genuine pity for all of humanity. He is tortured by anguished concern for those he loves and he experiences an occasional tug of sympathy for his enemies. But, speaking purely and solely for Popski, it's his finding that once somebody goes and starts a war the most exciting and satisfactory place to be is right in the middle of it.

In this attitude we fear he's anything but unique. The male animal being what he is, his intellectual and moral abhorrence of war is often tempered by an emotional acceptance of war. Provided that he has come home intact to the same family he left behind, almost any soldier of any nationality is apt to remember

87

his personal moments of heroism and pleasure long after he has forgotten his personal moments of suffering and fear. And if men coming back from war tend to be optimists after the fact, men going away to war tend to be optimists before the fact – and to an even greater degree.

We're not quite gloomy enough to believe that, because of this, war and human nature are inseparable. Neither, on the other hand, are we quite cheerful enough to believe that human nature alone is a defense against war.

So long as wars continue to get started men will continue to fight them through – and even find a perverse and highly exaggerated satisfaction in remembering how they did it. To say that war has become impossible merely because "the common people won't stand for another war" is to ignore one of history's most chilling and inescapable lessons. Until the world enters an entirely new moral climate, the prevention of war will remain a problem for our intelligence. If our intelligence fails us to the point where the shooting breaks out again there will be no scarcity of cannon fodder.

JOHN BAYNE MACLEAN, 1862-1950

(November 1, 1950)

If it observed the formalities this editorial would be enclosed in a black border. In the severe and narrow sense of that narrowest of words it concerns a death – the death of Lieutenant-Colonel John Bayne Maclean.

It's our feeling nevertheless that the magazine to which he gave his name cannot, in simple reality, concede the death of John Bayne Maclean. For as we mourned him the parts of him that lived were as close and challenging as tomorrow's deadline or the next stack of proofs. One of our editors had just left on a trip around the world to look, as a Canadian, at sundry trouble spots and try to discern what special meanings they hold for Canadians. One of our writers had just returned from a trip across Canada during which he talked to hundreds of teen-agers and tried to find out what the next generation is doing and thinking and hoping. Other people who work here were judging the two thousand entries in a contest for Canadian fiction writers. The presses were getting ready to roll on stories about a new Canadian fighting plane, a famous Canadian actor, a woman who runs a celebrated Canadian restaurant, a successful Canadian salesman and the mayor of a small Canadian town.

We who work for it are only too conscious that *Maclean's Magazine* often falls short of its founder's vision. We believe the vision itself – first seen at a time when there were no Canadian periodicals speaking to a general audience of Canadians on Canadian terms – was a great one. We believe that Canada has grown in stature in direct proportion to the growth of its national voice and that in pioneering a new, and for many years unprofitable, outlet for our national voice Colonel Maclean followed the highest ideals of public service.

John Bayne Maclean founded *Maclean's Magazine* – forerunner of three other national magazines and companion of three dozen business papers – at a time when doing so seemed neither sensible nor safe. Sixty-three years ago he quit a job as a seven-dollar-a-week reporter on a Toronto paper and started a small periodical publishing house of his own. By 1911 his largest and most profitable publication was *Busy Man's Magazine,* the original digest. But although *Busy Man's Magazine* was a highly successful venture commercially, it was jettisoned because it did not offer a medium through which Canadians could write and hear about Canadian affairs, Canadian attitudes and Canadian traditions. Its successor, *Maclean's,* lost heavily before it won acceptance. It won acceptance, finally, because John Bayne Maclean tried to teach it to speak up but not to speak stridently – in a voice sometimes hungry with aspiration, sometimes angry with self-criticism, more often as low and casual as the voice of next-door neighbours chewing the fat over a sunset. Over the long haul he sought to prove or disprove nothing except that understanding comes with knowledge.

That is why, as we honor him and mourn him, we cannot quite bring ourselves to believe that he is dead. Perhaps somewhere in this issue of the magazine that bears his name there will be a sentence or a phrase that will cause some young man or woman to believe that Canada is a better or more interesting place than he or she had realized, or that something is amiss in Canada that he or she must try to fix. Perhaps in time some small new better thing will come of that small new stirring of awareness.

And John Bayne Maclean, who is said to have died one day before his 88th birthday, will be embarked on the 89th year of a valiant and fruitful life.

FAITH, THE FINEST CHRISTMAS PRESENT

(December 15, 1950)

The most hopeful thing you can say about Christmas, as of Christmas, 1950, is that it's a miracle that hasn't jelled.

After one thousand nine hundred and fifty Christmases there is still no evidence to show that the weaker and baser parts of human nature are any less weak or base than they were before the first Christmas. It might be argued that the better parts of human nature are better, but the point cannot be proved.

What went wrong? Is it necessary to admit that – excluding the small change of roast turkey and purple ties – the currency of Christmas is too big for mortal hands to grasp? Is it necessary to admit that whatever it has to offer us in the celestial future, Christmas can improve our earthly present only by the measure of a few special acts of generosity or a few rich hours staked out once a year on a calendar?

We are certain that Christmas, even within its earthly limitations, was meant to mean more than that. One of the first and unmistakably specific promises it held forth was good will and peace on earth. The prophet Isaiah, an excessively gloomy person in the main, foretold the first Christmas, long, long before it happened, and painted a vision of grandeur before which humanity trembled. "Your covenant with death shall be disannulled," Isaiah promised, "and your agreement with hell shall not stand."

With an offer like that before us – to be had for the taking, any Christmas and all Christmases and on all the days between Christmases – why do we keep turning out backs? You don't have to be a prophet to sense that the offer is good and valid. You don't have to be an accountant to know what side the bargain's on. You don't have to have a religion to know that Christ talked the soundest kind of common sense. If you only believe that two and two make four, you must also believe that the world would be a better and safer and happier place if its inhabitants could be persuaded to live by the Sermon on the Mount.

These are the "logical" and "practical" arguments in favor of Christianity. And it is precisely because we have put so much store in the "practical" and "logical" sides of the Christian ideal that its practical and logical benefits have been so slender.

The logic which tells us that to practice Christianity is good also tells us that to practice Christianity is dangerous – unless you can get a guarantee that most of your neighbours are practicing it too. The logic which tells us there must be a God tells us not to put ourselves to too much inconvenience to follow His teachings, just in case it turns out that there isn't a God after all. The logic that tells us to love and trust our fellow men also warns us to watch our overcoats.

Fencing an ideal as sublime as Christmas with logic is in itself illogical, as illogical as trying to play "Adeste Fideles" on a toy drum.

We'll never realize the promise of Christmas until we learn that when you try to make a thing work for two thousand years on logic and still haven't got it working right, the logical thing to do is to try making it work on faith.

WHY AREN'T THERE ANY CRACKPOTS ON THE CANADA COUNCIL?

(May 25, 1957)

When we first looked at the make-up of the newly-formed Canada Council, our immediate reaction was one of bewilderment. We had thought, perhaps naïvely, that any group appointed to nourish such an unorthodox field as the arts would contain a few wild spirits. But the present group seems the epitome of orthodoxy.

Is the Council a board of directors for a trust fund of a hundred million dollars? Or is it a band of bold adventurers determined to see that talented but poverty-stricken writers, painters, musicians and actors have a chance to do the best work they are able to do while still eating?

We do not pretend to know the answer and for the moment we're withholding judgement. Certainly there is not a single member of the Council who could individually be challenged on the grounds of responsibility, competence and public spirit. It may be that in the entire history of the human race no group has ever been assembled with so mountainous a weight of respectability. But, while no individual appointee needs apologizing for or explaining, their portrait as a group is at least a little puzzling. They are all such completely sane and solid citizens, chiefly noted for their probity and solvency, that it is difficult to see them marching with hampers and words of comfort into the nation's artistic garrets.

We have always had the anti-social notion that there's nothing altogether wrong with garrets. Start cluttering them up with calf's-foot jelly and nourishing chicken broth and they tend to lose the character and virtue of garrets, which are by no means negligible.

But, like most Canadians, we're quite prepared to wait and see in spite of our private reservations. The concept behind the Canada Council is good and decent and potentially rewarding to us all.

We earnestly trust the men and women in charge of it will begin their task with the knowledge that they have two strikes against them. In the mass they have such a sane and corporate aspect that the long-hairs, and indeed a number of conservative and quite rational intellectuals, can't wait to start sticking pins in them. And if they begin squandering that hundred million dollars on grimy, unsuccessful violin players they will get an equally bad name in the board rooms and ivied halls from which they sprang.

If the Cabinet had thought to include just one tame lunatic or down-at-the-heels sculptor among these impeccable dignitaries, their task would have been immensely easier. They'd have had at least one tiny voice urging them to live dangerously and at least one scapegoat for their follies.

As it is they are facing certain trouble and contumely from all quarters of the wind. We salute them for the patriotic impulse in which they undertook their assignment and hope, even if we cannot predict, that they'll make out well.

THE ELECTION AND DEMOCRACY*

(June 22, 1957)

The recent federal election – as a trial rather than as a verdict – offers little cause for pride or for dismay.

No one got excited about this election. Perhaps it created a third as much comment as the latest television performance of Elvis Presley – certainly no more. It may well be that as much time was spend this month in marking ballots as in picking up trading stamps – maybe. One safe statement is that the mysterious, complicated, precious and precarious institution called democracy once more has proved to be roughly as enthralling to the average voter as a case of fallen arches.

Here, an optimist might hope, is the real beauty of democracy. You can take it or leave it alone. But without quarreling with that serene notion we feel required to set down two or three reminders of where the system of government called democracy came from and what it really means.

Democracy, alas, is not a good thing in itself. One of the most persuasive thinkers of our time, the late H.L. Mencken, used to argue that it was no more than a trap for boobs. The thirteenth edition of *The Encyclopaedia Britannica* reminds us that: "According to Aristotle, democracy is the perverted form of the third form of government. . . . Aristotle's restriction of democracy to bad popular government, i.e. mob-rule, or as it has sometimes been called 'ochlocracy,' was due to the fact that the Athenian democracy had in his day degenerated far below the ideals of the fifth century, when it reached its zenith under Pericles. . . . Since Aristotle's day the word has resumed its natural meaning, but democracy in modern times is a very different thing from what it was in its best days in Greece and Rome. . . . The population became too large and the distance too great for regular assemblies of qualified citizens. . . . The essence of modern representative government is that the people does not govern itself, but periodically elects those who shall govern on its behalf."

In this, we fear, there is a bleak truth that cannot be escaped. Democracy – unless we make it work and unless we make our elected delegates work at making it work – is no better a system of government than the rankest dictatorship.

*Editor's Note: This is the famous Maclean's *"election editorial" which erroneously assumed that the Liberals would be re-elected and appeared on the news-stands the day after John Diefenbaker swept them out of office.*

For better or for worse, we Canadians have once more elected one of the most powerful governments ever created by the free will of a free electorate. We have given that government an almost unexampled vote of confidence, considering the length of its term in office. It could easily be forgiven for accepting this as a mandate to resume the kindly tyranny it has exercised over parliament and the people for more than twenty years.

But now, somehow, we must hope that our new government, encyclopaedias notwithstanding, will give up the idea once and for all that "the people does not govern itself but periodically elects those who shall govern on its behalf." For if this philosophy is to seize the Canadian people and to remain the blueprint for Canadian governments, then we might as well confess that in its essential meaning for Canada, democracy is not much more than a high-flown foreign word borrowed from a far-off foreign people.

WE WERE DEAD WRONG ON YOUR VOTE

(July 6, 1957)

"For better or for worse, we Canadians have once more elected one of the most powerful governments ever created by the free will of a free electorate. We have given that government an almost unexampled vote of confidence, considering the length of its term in office. It could easily be forgiven for accepting this as a mandate to resume the kindly tyranny it has exercised over parliament and the people for more than twenty years."

The above collector's item, displayed prominently on our editorial page, began reaching the readers of this magazine on the day after the recent federal election. Although it has been received with a flattering degree of attention, it would be a serious exaggeration to say that we are proud of having created it. To get down to brass tacks, and to borrow from our own orotund prose of previous date, it represents an almost unexampled case of editorial fat-headedness. We consider it worthy of a place in our trade's chamber of horrors beside the newspaper headlines and magazine covers which in November 1948 greeted Thomas E. Dewey as the new President of the United States some hours and days after he had been liquidated by Harry Truman.

We apologize for our error, which was of two dimensions. In the first and simplest dimension it was an attempt to beat a deadline with a crystal ball. In the second and more important, it was – glory be! – an altogether too pessimistic guess about the temper of the Canadian people in this prosperous year of 1957. Like the Liberals, we underestimated this nation's capacity for indignation, its willingness, when driven far enough by the trustee concept of government, to tear up the profit statement and throw it right in the trustees' remote, benevolent faces. Like the Liberals, we doubted that any decisive part of the population was prepared to turf out the safe and sane management of the last twenty-two years just because it had grown wilful and autocratic and openly disdainful of certain rights which, when compared with material well-being, can seem pretty wispy and ephemeral.

We were dead wrong. Beneath those mountains of ore the heartbeat of Canada may flutter and grow sluggish. The oil and natural gas coursing through its arteries may leave their dangerous deposits of fat. But when we suspect that the roots of our democratic nationhood have been placed in jeopardy, we can still be as healthy and lean and tough-minded as the circumstances require.

In this reassuring discovery there are new challenges and opportunities not only for the Conservatives but for the Liberals themselves. Their contributions to our nationhood and our growth – while in power and while in opposition – have been incalculable. It would be singularly ungrateful to deny those contributions now. In power or in opposition there is every reason to believe and hope that in the months and years ahead they will again be a vital force – almost an indispensable force, almost indispensable but not quite – in helping us to extract the greatest possible good from our good system of government. During their last twenty-two years in office they helped to give the Canadian people many things, material fortune and a high place in the councils of the world not being the least of these. It was their mistake, as we earnestly pray it will be their lesson, that they forgot for a few fatal years to give us something infinitely more important – a sense of full participation in our own affairs.

LOVE IS SOMETHING MORE THAN SEX BUT YOU'D NEVER KNOW IT NOWADAYS

(August 17, 1957)

The Roman Catholic Auxiliary Bishop of Toronto, F.A. Marrocco, recently uttered some wise, if mildly debatable words. This, in part, is what he said: "False values of living have infected the idea of marriage and the meaning of love has been reduced to sexual satisfaction. Thousands do not know how to love in terms of personality rather than in terms of lumps of flesh.

"The mother should be the heart of the family. It would help the return to this concept if we stopped thinking of women as lumps of flesh. It would help, too, if women stopped acting like lumps of flesh."

Bishop Marrocco, we think, takes an unnecessarily gloomy view, if not of the human race's self-control, of its powers of imagination. Many a rose-lipped maiden and many a lightfoot lad are lacking poets to clothe their wicked thoughts in magic. Not every royal satyr can invoke the Songs of Solomon or every Falstaff command a Shakespeare to exalt his lust. But we doubt that any woman, in wedlock or out, however dull of mind or slatternly of soul, couldn't do a little bit better than lump of flesh in defining her own physical attractions. We doubt that any man, however cloddish and insensitive, could look on any woman as a lump of flesh and still have any continuing romantic interest in her.

But for all his understatement, Bishop Marrocco has made a statement that is essentially true. The meaning of love – both the reality and the word – has been sadly confused and corrupted. Viewed either as an instrument of human expression or as a condition of human relations, love is not only blind but almost mute. It has lost its ancient peal and dignity; the song-writers, moviemakers and magazine authors have made so free and easy with it that its best and oldest usages are gone. True, it is still barely permissible to use the word, in certain limited contexts, outside the orbit of sex. It is all right, for instance, for a man to love another man and admit it provided they are closely related or widely apart in ages. It is all right for preachers to talk about love in the old-fashioned universal and Christian sense; it's one of their remaining special privileges. But with such exceptions it's pretty generally accepted that if love doesn't rhyme with dove it doesn't count.

This is far more serious than a mere mutation of language. Because they have been betrayed into believing that love must rhyme with dove and never rhyme with anything else, millions of people go into marriage expecting both far too much of it and far, far too little. Lured into the belief that love is desire and nothing more and that desire is love and nothing less, they lose the best of both worlds.

(July 5, 1958)

Most readers of this magazine are familiar with the name and work of Lionel Shapiro. For nearly twenty years, until his recent death, he was the chief foreign correspondent of *Maclean's*. In that capacity, he wrote almost a hundred articles from the battle-fields of the last war and from many parts of the strewn world it left behind. He increased his reputation, which was an international one, through his novels, plays, motion pictures and personal appearances as a speaker and broadcaster. He was among the most successful of all Canadian writers. He was also among the best informed, the most gifted and the most perceptive. He was a passionate Canadian who, for all the fame and rewards he won in other parts of the world, never considered giving up his Canadian citizenship, his Canadian residence or his Canadian identity.

Lionel Shapiro's public record speaks so well for him that the conventional testimonials to his personal quality seem anti-climactic. Indeed, as he himself would have been the first to point out, they may not even be in order. Shapiro was not, in the ordinary sense, the Sterling Character or the Grand Chap who usually appears as the hero of obituary notices. He was egotisti-cal, neurotic, melancholy, obstinate and generally difficult. One of his friends had a favorite and no doubt made-up story about him that he used to tell in Lionel's presence. "But John," Shapiro would say, "here I've been talking about myself for two hours. How about you talking about me for awhile?"

Shapiro was first, throughout and at the end Lionel Shapiro. Everything he did proclaimed his individuality; he wrote in his own way, he lived in his own way, he died in his own way; there was no conceivable chance of mistaking him for anyone but himself.

I can remember him saying, "I'm going to take a week off and write a play for NBC." He wrote it and NBC bought it and produced it. I can remember him saying, "I'm going to take two weeks off and write a short story for the *Saturday Evening Post*." This, by the way, was before he had ever written a short story for anybody, but the *Saturday Evening Post* bought and published it. He phoned me when the Literary Guild offered to buy his last novel. "I don't think I'll accept," he said. "If we wait another few weeks the Book of the Month Club will probably take it for August." That's what happened.

In the time I have been at *Maclean's,* working with him not as a friend and frequently companion of our days as war correspondents but in the impersonal and sometimes tough relationship between a writer and an editor, it is my assessment that his batting average was well over .950.

For the last two months of his life Shapiro knew that he was certain to die in a very short time. He had had one operation for cancer. Because he was, in every circumstance, the kind of reporter who had to know the truth, he discovered from his doctors that there might be a recurrence and that a recurrence, so far as these things can be foretold by mortals, would be fatal. When the recurrence came he knew exactly what it meant. No one tried to deceive him about it. He did not try to be deceived.

He was in a position that many others have faced with tranquility and courage. In his case there was one circumstance that called for extra courage. The person to whom he had been closest throughout his life, the person whose sympathy and comfort would have meant the most to him in his last weeks, was the one person he felt he must not confide in. His mother, with whom he had shared a great and tender devotion throughout his life, was seriously ill too under the care of nurses in the Montreal apartment which was their home. Sharpiro was convinced that if he told her of his own condition she might find the shock too difficult to bear. So when he left their apartment for the last time to take the short, absurdly convenient taxi journey to the hospital, he simply told her that he was having trouble with his new novel, that his New York publishers wanted him to go down and discuss it and work on it there. He had taken his mother's resident nurse into his confidence and so he was able to telephone several times a week, ostensibly from the St. Moritz Hotel in New York but really from the Montreal General Hospital, and wish his mother good night.

It was in the same spirit that he talked with and heard from some of the people who knew about his sickness. He received and very much valued messages from people as eminent as Lord Alexander, Lord Montgomery and the Canadian generals Crerar, McNaughton and Simonds. And although he was not able to see more than a half-dozen visitors and although he could not use a typewriter or a pen or pencil, he still managed to write two or three letters on the dictaphone that had been placed at the side of his bed. And into the dictaphone he put a short and much-interrupted account of his last experiences and thoughts. As a good reporter he had known for some time that many promising new drugs and chemicals were being developed in the fight against cancer. He asked his doctors to use as many of them as they could on him, no matter how hopeless and painful they might be. And during the two months when he stood almost at every single hour at the threshold between life and death he found the strength and resolution to pick up the mouthpiece of the dictaphone and get into it some of his observations of what it was like. Once he said, "This is the most exhilarating thing that has happened to me personally since the war. Happy ending or not, I am excited by the chance to view this struggle between the scientists and the doctors and the disease inside of me."

In the end the disease got the better of his body, but it never came close to conquering his spirit. I was one of the few visitors he was allowed to have and I went from Toronto to Montreal several times in those last weeks to talk with him. In his years of good health and prosperity he was one of the most notorious and chronic worriers who ever set foot on earth. A hangnail, a cold in the head, a lukewarm letter from an editor, or a drop of fifty cents in the stock of Imperial Oil or Royal Bank could set him off on a lament of several days and positively Biblical gloom. But he was much too proud to let himself be frightened by anything really dangerous. The last time I said good-by to him he said simply and calmly, "This is okay. Nothing is hurting much. I can handle it." And so he did – handled his life well and handled his death well and left them both with dignity.

THE LAND OF ETERNAL CHANGE

(June 25, 1955)

Their fiftieth official spring came this year to the provinces of Saskatchewan and Alberta as spring always comes there – full of new hopes and old anxieties, aglow with a thousand shades and forms of beauty of which only a few can be detected by a stranger, bursting with variety and surprise.

The dominant qualities, as they were even before the two provinces became provinces, are variety and surprise. To anyone whose notions of it have been acquired through movies or train windows, a close inspection of the West this spring would have brought mixed feelings of recognition and disbelief. On March 23, two days after the equinox, the southern wheatlands were digging themselves out of ten-foot snow-drifts. As April turned the corner into May, both provinces were sloshing through blizzards, followed in Saskatchewan by floods that reached disaster size.

But at last the gleaming prairie sun came out, apparently to stay, and now in June those magnificent *clichés,* the meadow lark and the crocus again offer their yearly paean of melody and fragrance. Although it is true that the melody now competes with the angry clatter of drill rigs and the fragrance is sometimes engulfed in the reek of petroleum fumes, there are other things that still have at least the appearance of timelessness. When the moon is out coyotes call longingly, as they did a thousand years ago, from the silver clumps of wolf-willow on the hillsides. On the golden faces of the Rockies mountain sheep and goats march primly up past the timber-line, as they did centuries before the first explorers. Other native creatures have seen fit, like the men and women who grew up there, to modify the interests and habitations of their ancestors. Magpies dart out of the chokecherry bushes and popular bluffs to snoop about the Christmas-trees and the pumps of seven thousand producing oil wells, and great stark ravens croak in the morning sunlight above the uranium mines north of Lake Athabaska.

For humans there have been large changes too. Their standard living unit is still a four-,five- or six-room farmhouse which may or may not have paint, may or may not have plumbing and may or may not have electricity. But since the war, the other pole of domestic architecture – the California suburb – has planted itself in all the major cities. The chief characteristic of this newest of all the West's new phenomena is the residents' apparent determination to be themselves and to let the neighbours be the same. The result, which reaches its climax in an Edmonton housing development called Glenora, is a wildly unfettered mixtured of shapes and colors: scale model castles-in-Spain cheek-to-jowl with plywood living-machines, plaster against clapboard, stucco against brick, aquamarine blue against coral pink, alligator green against daffodil yellow, midget minarets beside open-deck verandas.

It is not only the dwellings that change. Straw-stacks no longer burn on the prairie summer fallow. This year it is giant torches of gas that hiss and flame and break the black silence of the night sky. On the rims of the cities, where the last lonely street lamps used to mark the beginning of the open plain, the refineries with the marching lights of their cracking towers now stand guard like fairy battleships.

The belief that the West goes on repeating itself, mile after mile and year after year and generation after generation, has never stood up under close scrutiny. Neither has the belief that it is almost wholly populated by the same kind of people doing the same kind of thing for the same kind of reason. If you exclude the Indians, who were there at least three thousand years ago, the first substantial influx of permanent settlers began in 1870. It was led across what is now the Manitoba – Saskatchewan border by métis hunters, just defeated in the first Riel Rebellion and now seeking space, buffalo and freedom from the white man's red tape. Almost at once a great pincers movement began to envelop the half-breed hunters; missionaries pursuing them from the east to save their souls, whisky traders riding in from the south to swindle them out of their buffalo hides.

The next and largest wave of settlers – the English, the Irish and the Scots, the Americans and eastern Canadians, the Ukrainians and Germans, the Scandinavians, the Hungarians and Rumanians and Russians and Poles – had even more diverse origins and equally diverse reasons for coming. Some were drawn by fear, some by faith, some by ambition, some by greed, some by gullibility. The one statement that can be applied to all of them and all of their descendants is that they've seen a very great amount of history is a very short time. Men who trembled or rejoiced at the hanging of Louis Riel will still be alive in Saskatchewan this summer to tremble or rejoice at the opening of the fabulously rich Gunnar uranium mine. Homesteaders whose first saleable crop was whitened buffalo bones are now living in retirement on their oil royalties. Taxpayers who, a half century ago, had no real voice in their own government have lived to shake the country's whole political structure by electing the C.C.F. in Saskatchewan and Social Credit in Alberta. Half-broke dirt farmers who once had no choice but to sell their wheat for as little as the grain dealers cared to offer and to buy their groceries and fuel for as much as the retailers cared to ask are today the owners of a huge co-operative empire of elevators, stores, factories and even oil wells and a refinery.

In Alberta last February, I talked to William Hawrelak, an immigrant from the Ukraine, who remembered floating down the North Saskatchewan River on a raft fifty-seven years ago until he found the quarter section of free homestead land that suited him.

The place where he boarded the raft then had a population of a few hundred. It's now well beyond two hundred thousand. Its name is Edmonton, and its mayor is William Hawrelak's son, Bill Jr.

From the start, the story of the two provinces that were carved out of the Northwest Territories fifty years ago has been a story of the unexpected and the unknown. It must remain so for at least another fifty years, for Saskatchewan and Alberta represent a union whose fruit is unpredictable almost by definition – the union of a very old land with a very young people. Some of the land, the northern rocks of the Canadian Shield, is as old as any land in the world. The prairies are older than the Nile, older than the hills of Jerusalem, older than Galilee and the valley of the Jordan. And the people are just as spectacularly young. Among voluntary settlers and descendants of settlers, they are second in their newness to their home only to the modern Jews of Israel, and the Jews knew Israel centuries before they returned to it.

It took the old land many millions of years to hew out its rocks and mountains, to bury its twenty-ton lizards and flying dragons, to sift and grind its soil, to hide its lakes of inflammable ooze and its underground hills of coal and metal. It took the young people who came there a maximum of decades and a minimum of weeks to size up the land and guess how best to live with it. In reality they knew very little of what to expect from the climate, or what the soil would stand, or what lay secreted beneath the soil.

It was no accident that they were naïve and ill-informed. As the transcontinental railway pushed through the plains in the early 1880's it pushed through empty country. The whole prairie from Winnipeg west had only sixty thousand white inhabitants when the decade began. Halfway through the eighties the Dominion government had had fewer than twenty thousand takers for the free homesteads it had begun offering more than ten years earlier, and more than half of these had already abandoned their farms and gone back to Ontario or the U.S. The C.P.R. had no traffic for its railway and no buyers for its twenty-five million acres of land along the right of way. By the mid-nineties the expected wave of settlement still had shown no sign of coming. Clearly, unless something quick and drastic were done the rails would turn to rust and with them the dream of a Canadian nation stretching from coast to coast.

The needed and drastic thing was done, by a quick and drastic man named Clifford Sifton. Sifton was federal Minister of the Interior. His was the chief responsibility for trying to fill a void a third as large as Europe. During the years between 1896 and 1905 Sifton and the C.P.R. with some help from the Hudson's Bay Company, the Grand Truck Pacific and a few private colonization companies, staged the largest, noisiest and most successful medicine show in history. It covered two continents and was conducted in a dozen languages. Its message was simple and direct: Whatever ails you, come to Western Canada! In his role as chief barker, Sifton published millions of pamphlets extolling the free land of the Northwest Territories, and offering it gratis to anyone who could come and get it. In impressive rounded phrases worthy of a multilingual W.C. Fields, his literature cajoled the Swedes in Swedish, harangued the Germans in German, beguiled the French in French, coaxed the Hollanders in Dutch, wheedled the Norse in Norwegian.

The C.P.R. supported him by sending out equally persuasive pamphlets in Welsh, Gaelic, Danish and Finnish, as well as the more common Western languages. At one time Sifton had twenty-one advertising agencies working for him. He and the C.P.R. brought free-loading American editors to the prairies by the trainload. Successful Western farmers from Britain and the U.S. were sent back home, as guests of the Dominion government, to carry the gospel to their old neighbours. Sifton sold huge tracts of Canadian government land at giveaway prices to private colonization companies, then paid them a bounty out of the Dominion treasury for every settler they could produce – five dollars for the head of a family, two dollars each for women and children.

For every worthy human aspiration, and for some that weren't so worthy, the new paradise offered the virtual certainty of fulfillment. Poor? Where else could you acquire a hundred and sixty acres of land for a ten-dollar registration fee? Where else would a railroad take you halfway across a continent for six dollars? Opposed by conscience to military service? What other nation would offer conscientious objectors a guarantee against conscription? In a hurry? This from a pamphlet that bore Sifton's name: "The shrewd and sturdy settler who plants a little capital and cultivates it can, with due diligence, in a few years, produce a competency." Lazy? J. Obed Smith, one of Sifton's departmental assistants, assured the prospective immigrant, "He can make his crop in less than four months."

Sifton and his associate spellbinders answered possible hecklers in advance. Schools inadequate, sir? "Educationists," a Sifton circular announced solemnly in 1903, "assert the school system of the Northwest Territories is equal, if not superior, to that of any other country." Communications unsatisfactory, sir? "Excellent railway facilities, admirable postal arrangements." Greater opportunities, my dear sir, in the United States? As a minister of the crown, Sifton doubtless felt he could not personally denigrate a friendly nation. The C.P.R. handled the question with a deft effusion of crocodile tears: "The decadent condition of many American farms is no doubt due to the prevalence of the tenant system."

One C.P.R. circular, aimed directly at attracting immigrants from the U.S.A., borrowed the satisfied-user technique so popular with pill manufacturers. Typical headings above the testimonials read: "Would not Return to Indiana", "Dakota Farmer Succeeded Without Capital", "Prefers the Weyburn District to the States", "Easily Earns Holiday Trips to Ohio."

The cold prairie winters and the hot dry prairie summers were never a serious embarrassment to Sifton, who contented himself with calling them "splendid." To have said anything less would have been, according to the relaxed idiom of the times, to have tampered with the truth. Even as late as 1910 by which time a good deal more evidence about Western weather was on the record, not all of it favourable, a Grand Trunk pamphlet trumpeted, "The time has probably passed when the impression can exist that Western Canada has a forbidding climate. Such fabrications have been put forth freely in the past by designing persons, but the greatest factors in advertising the delightful features of the climate, which quite submerge the few slight drawbacks, are the people already settled there, prosperous and happy. The summers are ideal in every respect with sufficient rainfall properly distributed, and when winter sets in with its bracing dry atmosphere and clear days, there is nothing to dread, but much to enjoy in this season of meeting friends and indulging in the sports and pastimes of the season."

The siren song was heard halfway around the world. Those earthy mystics, the Doukhobors, heard it in Russia and in a single month seven thousand of them streamed off the gangplanks at Saint John and boarded the colonist cars for Winnipeg and the central plains of Saskatchewan. Heartwick Ukrainians, without land and without a country, heard it under the flag of Austria, under the flag of the Imperial Czar, even under the flag of Brazil. They were soon to be Western Canada's second largest racial group, second only to the Anglo-Saxons. Cockneys heard it in the crowded mews of Hackney. Members of the minor gentry heard it on the minor estates of Surrey and invited their younger sons into the study for a serious talk about the future. Ontario farm boys heard it as their time grew near for leaving home. So did ranchers from Texas, Oklahoma and Montana, cramped by fences.

Once the people started coming, Sifton did his best to retrieve his promises. At the railway terminals and along the staging routes, the Dominion government opened ninety immigration halls and staging camps, where bunks, cookstoves, surveyors' maps, advice and interpreters were available free of charge. By 1901 Saskatchewan's population was more than ninety thousand and Alberta's more than seventy thousand and in the next ten years these figures were quintupled. The dream of a nation had been redeemed.

The cost of its redemption and its reaffirmation in the half century since 1905 bore no relation to the estimates on the immigration folders. The ancient land proved alternately hospitable and cranky, kind and savage, benign and spiteful. Thousands of the settlers were wholly ignorant of agriculture. Even the relatively experienced Europeans knew little about farming large acreages; to them the basic tools were the grub hoe, the scythe, the hand flail and winnow and the wooden plow. Erosion and soil drifting were as foreign to the settlers' thoughts as nuclear energy. Drought, hail and autumn frost were unheard of – at least in the sunny folklore of the Department of the Interior. Grasshoppers, rust and weeds did not begin to appear north of the border until well after the turn of the century.

Thus the pioneers were ripe for ambush. Their mistakes were frequent, and ranged from the tragic to the bizarre. So did the vindictiveness of nature and the land. Of the first four white people to die in Saskatoon, two froze to death in blizzards, one drowned in the Saskatchewan River and the other died of exhaustion after fighting a prairie fire. In Alberta in 1906-7 the Chinook failed. The owners of the big ranches had no hay for their herds, for they had come to depend on the soft winter wind to uncover the uncut grass. Cattle and horses starved or froze by the tens of thousands. The Bar-U Ranch alone lost twelve thousand head. In 1903, a year of blizzards and bright sunshine, hundreds of horses went snow-blind and lost their lives by tumbling over precipices or blundering into gullies. A physician attached to the famous Barr colony, a mass pilgrimage of English families to Saskatchewan in 1903, complained that he spent most of his time patching up self-inflicted axe wounds.

The individual settlers' ideas of how to equip themselves for life on the frontier were often imaginative but odd. Not long ago Ray Coates, who arrived from England in 1903, recalled with amusement that he had come armed with dumb-bells, boxing-gloves and other muscle-building devices. At least one somewhat earlier arrival is known to have brought a case of Gold Cure, a contemporary remedy for alcoholism. Georgina Binnie-Clark, a spinster lady of quality, arrived in the Qu'Appelle Valley in 1905 with an expensive and ornate bathtub. She discovered that to fill it she would have to haul water three hundred yards, a pail at a time, from a well barely capable of supplying enough drinking water, so she sold the tub to another English lady, who discovered that she would have to haul water two miles to fill it. It ended up as a storage bin for seed. Mrs. Robert Wilson, of Bienfait, Saskatchewan, recently recalled a disaster that may have been unique; a horse once fell through the roof of her family home, a sod hut which her father had built on a hillside.

Their loyal children and their sentimental grandchildren have tried to enforce the tradition that the pioneers endured their troubles, large and small, with unfailing cheerfulness and courage. The theory is only partly supported by the written history of the period and by a cross-check with almost any of the thousands of men and women who lived through it and are still here to tell about it. Not long ago, I talked to a retired Leduc farmer named Luke Smith, born Lucan Smtz in Poland. Smith arrived in Halifax nearly sixty years ago. His pocket was picked aboard the ship and he docked without a penny. He borrowed two dollars from the fellow immigrant who was later to be his father-in-law and with that and his railway ticket he got to Edmonton. He went to work as a railway section-hand at a dollar a day and after four years had saved enough money to make the down payment on a quarter section of land.

It took years to clear the land but he sustained himself by selling willow posts and firewood. By 1946 he had every right to call himself a success. He had raised and seen to the education of five children and he had a good farm with good crops, good cattle and good buildings. A man called in one day and offered him five dollars, plus a per-barrel oil royalty for his mineral rights. Smith took it like a shot. ("I drilled twenty times for water and got nothing. So who's going to find oil? I was so glad about the five dollars I took it to town and bought a bottle of whisky.") A few months later the Leduc discovery-well came in and Smith's next-door-neighbour sold his mineral rights for $200,000. If Smith had any regrets on this score, they were not serious enough to remember; his per-barrel oil royalties still run as high as $3,000 a month and Luke and his vigorous, smiling wife give all but $200 of this to their children and grandchildren.

Just before Franklin Arbuckle and I left the cottage to which Luke and Mrs. Smith have retired, I asked a fairly routine question: "Were you as happy in the early days as you are now?" I half expected a routine answer about the joys and satisfactions of hardship and struggle honourably endured. Luke Smith and his wife have richly earned the right to clothe their memories in sentiment. But Luke was silent for several seconds, his strong, serene face deep in thought. Then he looked up gravely toward the kitchen doorway where Mrs. Smith stood with a dishcloth and the last of the supper dishes. The look they exchanged clearly said: This question must be answered truly, but is it best that the man answer it, or the woman? At last it was Mrs. Smith who answered. "He cried lots of times," she said with quiet dignity. "They all did."

In one way or another nearly everyone who was farming in Saskatchewan or Alberta fifty years ago says the same thing. In the last few years the provincial archives office of Saskatchewan has been asking original settlers to put their experiences on paper in order to flesh out the sparse printed records of the time. To the questions, "How did you learn farming?", Frank Baines, of Saltcoats, replied succinctly: "By trial and error, with large portions of the latter." R. E. Ludlow recalled, "Nobody had nothing, and we all used it." Mrs. May Davis, who came to Canada from England in 1883, drew a haunting picture of the finality with which so many people committed all their earthly hopes into what for so many of them was a literal void. "I can most particularly remember one poor sick-looking woman who was coming to Canada to join her husband, who had left England some months before. She had seven little boys with her, the youngest a baby at her breast. At our last sight she was on the wharf at Halifax, seated on a box of her 'effects,' waiting for her husband to come and claim them all. Did he come, I wonder – oh, but surely! – and where did they go and what became of them all? Perhaps by now one of those poor shabby little fellows has his name on the roster of Canada's famous men. Who can say? This is a land of opportunity and it is all a long, long time ago."

The society that took shape was one of the most heterogeneous in human history. Its axis of advance was along the main line of the C.P.R., and later along the C.P.R.'s branch lines and on the lines of its competitors. But the land immediately adjoining the right of way soon ran out or priced most buyers out of the market. As they fanned out from steel, by Red River cart, bull train or covered wagon and sometimes on foot, the Europeans tended to move north, where there were wood and water, no less important than soil and equally hard to come by in most of their native lands. The Americans, Eastern Canadians and English, Irish and Scots concentrated on the open prairie, where the treeless ground was ready for the plow.

In the first generation they set up islands bounded by language. Sometimes some special objective or special philosophy strengthened the ties of race. Saskatoon was founded as a temperance colony by a group of Toronto Methodists and as late as 1890 a man who wanted to buy a lot there had to agree not to "manufacture, buy, store, sell, barter, exchange, receive or give away or in any way deal in or use, possess or have intoxicating liquors or stimulants."

In the eighties, before Sifton's time, a group of French aristocrats settled near Whitewood, in what is now southern Saskatchewan. Their purposes were to lead a civilized life and to make expenses by engaging in forms of trade that would not have been considered appropriate to men of their class in France. From Paris they imported *pâté,* truffles and fine wines for their tables; servants for their kitchens and drawing rooms; hunting dogs for their kennels; fashionable hats and gowns for their ladies; white gloves and top hats for themselves. It was one of the memorable experiences of a memorable era to see the Marquis de Roffignac, M. le Comte Soras, M. le Comte Beaudrap and M. le Baron van Brabant sweeping across the still almost virgin plain in their shining imported phaetons drawn by their blooded horses, their liveried footmen sitting stiffly in attendance, their wives and daughters beside them smiling demurely beneath silk parasols. Unfortunately, the counts had not reckoned with a fact that later residents of Saskatchewan have found painfully obvious; as a home of industry, even of small industry, the thinly settled base of the

Palliser Triangle just doesn't make sense. The counts tried manufacturing brushes, sugar and Gruyère cheese. One of them attempted to raise and tin chicory, although the nearest sizeable market for chicory was back in France. One by one they lost their ruffled satin shirts and went home, disenchanted but uncomplaining. Many of the domestic servants they had brought out from France stayed behind; their descendants are still there, most of them prospering modestly on their farms.

Another eddy of elegance flourished for a while at Cannington Manor in south-east Saskatchewan no more than a hundred miles from the community farms where, a few years later, Doukhobors from Russia were to harness their wives and daughters to wooden plows. The founder of the Cannington colony was a retired British Army officer named Edward M. Pierce. In the early eighties, Pierce lost most of his capital in a bank failure and decided that if he was to live out his remaining years as a landed English gentleman, he would have to do it in Canada, where land was free. Pierce bought a team of oxen and drove his wife, their eight children and their furniture forty miles south of steel from Moosomin. He opened a private school and sent back advertisements to the English papers offering to teach farming, as well as the standard subjects, for a hundred pounds a year, including board and lodging.

His prize pupils were the three Beckton boys, Billie, Ernest and Bertie, grandsons of a Manchester cotton baron. The Beckton brothers who grew up as lean, languid bloods with drooping Mark Twain mustaches, remained to build their own estate. The main residence was of stone and had twenty-two rooms, including a billiard room. There were separate quarters for the servants, who included two valets. There was a gatehouse and a games-house, a large stable with hardwood and brass fittings, a private racetrack and tennis-courts. The Becktons imported thoroughbred horses and brought over two steeplechase jockeys from England. They tried to raise fighting roosters, but their first imported game-birds froze to death. They held fox-hunts and the house parties they threw at Christmas sometimes lasted three weeks.

With the Pierce and Beckton families as its lodestar, the hamlet gradually attracted other permanent settlers from England. There were enough young men to make up a cricket eleven and a rugger team good enough to play, and beat, the best in Winnipeg. There were enough handsome women in flowered frocks and big white hats to make the garden parties almost as much an event as the Beckton boys' race meetings. There were dances, chorales and amateur theatricals and of course a pretty little white Anglican church.

This Jane Austen world could not survive indefinitely in so improbable a setting. Captain Pierce died in 1888. The colony slowly scattered, leaving weeds to grow unchecked on the race-track and the grounds of the ageing mansions. Already, perhaps, the Captain had seen intimations of the failure of his dream, for one day, not long before his end, he looked out the window of his home to see seated in the front yard an Indian brave whom he recognized as Sha-wa-kal-coosh, son of Chief White Bear, whose reservation was nearby. Sha-wa-kal-coosh was dressed in the full splendour of his beads, feathers and ornamental moccasins and around his shoulders he wore a scarlet blanket. In the cradle of his arms he held a musket. It was not through any uneasiness, but simply because of a gentleman's natural reserve, that Captain Pierce did not immediately go out to ask Sha-wa-kal-coosh what he wanted. But as the day wore on and the Indian still squatted there immobile and expressionless, the Captain felt some relaxation of his social code might be permitted, so he sent one of his sons out to accost the brave. The son returned to say that Sha-wa-kal-coosh wished to trade his musket for Captain Pierce's eldest daughter, Lucy. Pierce had him shown off the grounds.

The outlines of the first conglomerate pattern of settlement are still clearly visible. There is scarcely a man or women living anywhere in Europe or North America who could not, somewhere in Saskatchewan or Alberta, find a sizeable community that speaks his language, sings his songs, and worships his gods. But he would still be first of all among Canadians. The fusion and assimilation of the West's unwieldy mixture of racial, religious, social and economic groups has been almost unbelievably rapid. With one notable exception it was accomplished without serious shock. Some eighteen hundred members of the Yorkton Doukhobor colony threw the whole country into confusion and dismay when, in 1902, they abandoned their community farms, turned their cattle loose and began marching the three hundred miles to Winnipeg, chanting prayers and hymns. Their exact reason was never fully established, for few of their leaders spoke English and those who did spoke in the mysterious symbols of the obsessed. Probably they had at least three main reasons: an intuitive belief that their messiah, Peter Verigin, who was then in Russia, would meet them somewhere on the way; a recent letter from Verigin condemning the cultivation of land and the ownership of cows and horses; a determination to seek out a climate warm enough to allow them to respect Verigin's injunction against the use of clothing.

The Mounted Police turned back the women and children at once. The men and boys, many of them barefoot, reach Minnedosa, a hundred and fifty miles from their starting point, before they too were rounded up by the police and returned to their homes by special train. For many more years the Doukhobors, with their constant revolts against sending their children to school, taking the oath of allegiance, or registering births, marriages and deaths, showed few signs of reaching a bare working agreement, much less a state of understanding, with their neighbours. Oddly enough they became easier to get along with after Verigin himself appeared on the scene. He ordered a relaxation of the more uncompromising articles of faith. This alienated the most fanatical of his followers, the barn-burning, disrobing Sons of Freedom, who left and thus transferred the "Doukhobor problem" from the prairies to British Columbia.

Other problems arose among and between the dozen other major ethnic groups, but before long they found a much more interesting and vital subject for reflection and debate than either race or religion. That was politics.

The link between politics and the way people live has always been more direct and visible and insistent on the prairies than elsewhere in Canada. In the early days of settlement, most farmers dealt directly with the government for their land. The government helped to decide where the railways would go and on such decisions the farmer could prosper within reach of his markets or break his heart and go bankrupt trying to make a living two or three days beyond steel. Governments of one kind or other – first Dominion and Territorial and then provincial and municipal – decreed where the roads and schools would be. In some years governments fixed the price of grain and even told the farmer how much of it he could grow. In the years of drought it was government that decreed what fraction of a pair of shoes per year each of the farmer's children should have, how many pounds of turnip and how many loaves of bread. In the years of plenty it is government's job to move the wheat and sell it. In the early stages of settlement governments began reserving mineral rights and it is almost always government that takes the lease money and royalties when oil is found on a man's farm.

A salaried worker in an Eastern city may be conscious of government only on the days when his family-allowance cheques come in or his income-tax deductions go out. The rural Westerner is conscious of it all the time, and his other convictions are likely to be less violent than his political convictions. When my family moved to a small Saskatchewan town in 1922, I was informed within two days that Sam Erumovitz, the local harness maker, was a Grit. It wasn't until several weeks later that someone mentioned he was also a Jew. When the Ku Klux Klan invaded Moose Jaw in the late 1920's trumpeting the doctrine of white supremacy it had no trouble getting people out to watch the burning of the fiery cross. It even managed to stir a submerged and almost forgotten current of race feeling and is often given credit for influencing the provincial election of 1929. But when the Klan sought to specify how it proposed to save the whites, it couldn't find anyone to save them from except a handful of Chinese restaurant owners. Some of these were employing non-Chinese waitresses. The Klan succeeded in bullying the Moose Jaw City Council into forbidding the practice. Shortly afterward it began to disband.

As the young people of the West have grown in understanding of each other, they have continued to grow in undertanding of the old land. Because of this, many of the people will be trying to predict, in this jubilee year, where they and the land are going and how and when they'll get there. Some of them will be knowing or lucky in their guesses. If past performance and the law of averages mean anything the vast majority will be just plain wrong.

For from the first day of the first white man to this June of 1955, the land has turned a different face to everyone. Three pioneer wheat growers recently recalled what they remembered best about the first trek into their homesteads. Fred Martin wrote about walking into the Qu'Appelle Valley when the rosebushes and morning glory vines were higher than his head. Cecil Angell told me of his memories of driving an ox team to his homestead near Saskatoon; the land had just been burnt over and was "rough, hummocky and black as ink." Oscar Anderson who packed into La Glace in the Peace River Country, told me of seeing dead horses standing upright in the muskeg of the Edson Trail.

The land, nature, the machine age and the law of supply and demand, have among them confounded prophets from the beginning. Sixty years ago it would have seemed impossible that the patient, essential ox could become obsolete, or forty years ago that the day would come when farmers would be selling good horses for meat. Thirty years ago the disappearance of the threshing gang would have seemed not much more likely than the disappearance of wheat. Twenty years ago, when the drought was into the seventh of its nine years, it would have been a feeble and tasteless joke to suggest that the farmers of Saskatchewan alone would lose nearly four hundred million dollars worth of grain because of too much rain in 1954 and that floods would threaten damage on an equal scale in 1955. Ten years ago, when rust was all but licked by new crossbreeds of wheat, only a writer of science fiction would have imagined that the rust fungus might counterattack by inventing its own crossbreed and thus make 1954 the worst rust year in history. Yet all these things happened.

And for all the Texas talk, oil still hasn't begun to make the West independent of agriculture. Four fifths of Saskatchewan's income still comes from the farm. Alberta's yearly farm production is still worth almost twice as much as its oil production.

Oil companies are spending a million dollars a day in the two provinces and still aren't taking nearly that amount out. This has provided tens of thousands of jobs, given business a general lift and, in Alberta, made provincial financing a simple problem in arithmetic. But the big fluctuations in income and well-being still follow wheat. Last year, as the exciting job went forward of proving up the new Pembina petroleum field south-west of Edmonton, it became apparent that this single new discovery contained close to three billion dollars worth of crude – more than Leduc and Redwater put together. Yet when they closed the books on that exceptionally good year for oil and exceptionally bad year for agriculture, retail sales for the province were down nearly ten per cent. In Saskatchewan the drop was twenty per cent. More than half the province's 112,000 farmers declared whole or partial crop failures and received relief under the Prairie Farm Assistance Act. No one is talking anything like ruin or looking over his shoulder for the unforgettable shadow of the thirties. But a great number of families have drifted back since last harvest to the farmhouses they deserted in the prosperous early fifties for the comforts of wintering in town. They have been putting cattle back in the barns they emptied to escape the monotony of twice-a-day chores, and some have been wondering audibly whether one-crop farming is good farming after all.

There are other riddles in the economic future of the two provinces, some of good omen, a few of bad omen, most of them just riddles. They involve such projects, underway or on the drawing boards, as a gas pipeline from Alberta to the East (still short of financial backing); a long-debated irrigation and power dam over the South Saskatchewan River (still not approved); recent discoveries of iron in the Peace River and potash near Saskatoon; and a projected pulp mill near Candle Lake, Saskatchewan. They involve such imponderables as the world price and the world demand for wheat and oil, both of which prairie producers are selling with some difficulty in a buyer's market.

The most maddening and intriguing riddle of all is the Athabaska Tar Sands, one of the greatest treasure stores ever beheld by man, worth far more than all of South Africa's diamonds and India's rubies and Canada's gold put together – and less than worthless until someone finds a way to mine them.

The tar sands lie deep in north-eastern Alberta. They are a thirty thousand square-mile deposit of individual drops of oil wrapped around individual grains of sand. In some places they are hidden by a thin overburden of rock, soil and scrub. In others they lie uncovered on the ground like vast black slabs of molasses candy. Some of Canada's and the world's best geologists have studied their potential. The most conservative estimate is that they contain a hundred billion barrels of crude – thirty-five times Canada's known reserves from other sources. Other estimates go as high as three hundred billion barrels, twice as much as the whole world's liquid reserves.

The private companies and government experts were experimenting with the Athabaska field fifty years before Leduc and Redwater came in. They proved long ago that the oil and sand can be separated, but no one has ever proved the job can be done at a practical cost. Bulldozers and steam shovels bog down in the rich goo like beetles caught in melting toffee. It is too soft to dynamite and not soft enough to move to a separating plant by tank truck or pipeline. Various engineers have tried to drill it, to beat it into a froth, to pump it, to blow it out by steam and to sink electrodes into it, crack the vapours underground and then condense them when they rise. Three years ago, a Calgary contractor named G.R.Coulson whirled a preserve jar full of the black mixture inside a washing machine. The oil broke away from the sand. A young mining man named S.R. Paulson got interested, formed a new company and gave Coulson enough backing to go on with his experiments in centrifugal separation. Recently Paulson's firm leased a small Alberta government separation plant forty miles downstream from Fort McMurray. Paulson says that with bigger and better scrapers and bulldozers he can lick the problem of collection, and that Coulson has already licked the problem of processing. The older oil companies, some of which are still drilling in the area "to protect their flanks," as one executive put it, are all sceptical. They agree that the oil is there in fabulous quantities. But the ones I talked to all said that until the price of crude goes much higher – perhaps twice as high as it is today – the tar sands will remain the tantalizing challenge they have been since the fur traders saw them more than a century ago.

The enigma of the tar sands is in the soundest, most enigmatic Western tradition. In the eight thousand miles I have traveled this year in Saskatchewan and Alberta, nearly everything I have seen has confirmed my boyhood belief, tested by countless excursions after gophers, learning,money, girls, and salvation, that anyone who thinks he knows what to expect next from that part of the world is an optimist. Not an optimist about the West itself – for there is a great deal of ground for optimism there – but an optimist about his own powers of divination.

One of the side-trips Franklin Arbuckle and I made took us as far from the West of 1905 as the West of 1905 is from the age of the dinosaur. We were in the mill at Eldorado, near Uranium City, where pitchblende ore is converted into a high-grade uranium salt by grinding it to powder, dissolving it in washing soda and then precipitating and filtering it. We had come into the massive square building out of a beautiful winter morning. Fresh snow clung to the evergreens on the hillside above Beaverlodge Lake and it was not hard to understand why Richard Barrett, who was just about to finish his tour of duty as mine manager, called the site "the prettiest mining camp God ever made."

Inside, at first, the mill looked as mills and factories often look to a layman; overpoweringly large and rather dull. But halfway around the passageway of ramps and platforms that runs beside the gigantic assembly line, we both began to notice the same thing. There were no people around. In the whole vast and suddenly eerie place I do not think we saw six men. The slowy turning worm-screws, the slowly turning drums, the whispering sluices, the immense red vats towering silently to the far-off roof, the whole mysterious forest of machines had achieved an almost terrifying self-sufficiency. It panted and whispered over its secret business in its own secret way, the stuff of Armageddon and the stuff of Utopia running side by side in its quiet blood stream. Once we saw two men dump a barrel of caustic soda into a vat and then go away. They were the only humans, except those looking after the power plant outside the main cavern and those carrying away the yellow uranium salt in small black barrels, who seemed in the least important to the enterprises of the machines. "The plant runs twenty-four hours a day," the mill manager told us. "Stopping it's a complicated business."

Kitty-corner from Uranium City, both geographically and historically, is the quiet and, I insist in defiance of all city slickers, pretty little town where I grew up. Its name is Oxbow.

How much Oxbow has changed in the twenty-five years since I last lived there depends entirely on the point of view. The population has increased one fifth to eight hundred. The Chinese restaurant has moved from the west side of the street to the east side and has installed neon lights. The poolroom still has two full-sized snooker tables and one Boston table. The second Boston table has been replaced by a three-quarter-size snooker table, an apparatus once considered fit only for the most miserable of hamlets. There are five churches instead of four. The old seven-room stone school-house still serves as a high school and right beside it they've built a shining new hundred-thousand-dollar public school and behind that there are dormitories where children from the country can get board and room for forty dollars a month. The tin-roofed skating and curling rink is still in use, and they've put new waiting rooms and a Legion hall on the end of it. Nobody meets the twice-a-day passenger trains any more except on business. The lobby of the Alexandra Hotel is no longer filled on Saturday afternoons by elderly philosophers and bridge players, but by small boys and girls waiting for television to come on from Minot, North Dakota. The rooms upstairs are occupied, not by drummers from Regina or Winnipeg but by seismic crews in search of oil. The grain elevators are not so high as they were when I lived there, and the sides of the Souris River Valley are not so steep; the young women are not quite so pretty and the young men are not quite so tall, but the deterioration may be in the observer rather than in the observed.

Although their parents are still there in healthy and happy profusion, there is almost no one of my generation there now. I was lucky enough, nevertheless, to meet one of my first friends.

Bob Pegg came back to Oxbow two years ago, not to visit but to stay. As it was with everyone who was finishing school when the Depression began, it had once been his greatest ambition to get away from Oxbow and to stay away forever. The unending years of dust, grasshoppers and rust and, above all, of the utter hopelessness of finding anything useful to do left very little choice. In these years the population of Saskatchewan dropped a hundred thousand and it still hasn't been restored; nearly everyone, at least those who were young, believed that Saskatchewan had no future. Bob Pegg escaped in 1934. He tried commercial fishing in the Northwest Territories and mining in Quebec. He joined the R.C.A.F., was shot down and spent two years as a prisoner of war.

After the war he started a sporting-goods business in the Maritimes in partnership with a friend, but the manufacturers couldn't supply them with enough stock to keep two men working so Bob pulled out.

"I wasn't ready to panic," he reflected. "There were lots of things I could have done and lots of places I could have gone. It was just that after wandering around for nearly twenty years I still didn't have a place I could call home. That reminded me that I could call Oxbow home if I wanted to."

Bob Pegg bought a half section of land on his D.V.A. credits and rented three more half sections. He read up on farming and asked advice about it. He decided not to become dependent on wheat. Last year his main crop was barley and he has a herd of seventy Hereford cattle. He had a good year. Over the long haul he thinks he has an outside chance of going broke, no chance at all of getting rich, and about a ninety-five per cent chance of living reasonably well as long as he does a reasonable amount of work.

We talked of these things as we drove down the long slope that tumbles off the edge of the town and falls past a dozen cuts and hidden ravines to the river. Over to the left there were fresh toboggan tracks on Blood Hill and on the right the sun was beginning to go down. This night the fading light was a faint purple; another night it might have been brick red or orange or a luminous, billowing black. "Maybe I shouldn't have left here in the first place," Bob said.

All over the two provinces, many of Bob Pegg's two million neighbours will be thinking their own long thoughts and trying to weigh the things they have to celebrate in this anniversary year.

There will be great variety in their answers – as much variety as in their beginnings and in their individual conditions and ways of life.

And when they try to forecast what the old land of the West holds for their children, they will again have to depend as much on individual intuition and individual experience as on the collected weight of history. A shepherd in the Cotswolds makes a reasonable deduction when he decides his son will probably be a shepherd in the Cotswolds too. That is what his great-grandfather was and his great-grandfather's great-grandfather before that. And so it is with a rice farmer in Japan or a weaver in India or to a somewhat lesser extent with a dairy farmer in Ontario or Quebec or a rancher in Texas. They and their ancestors have had time to learn about the land they live on, what it demands, what it will tolerate, what it conceals, what it will support. Barely a tenth of the mineral-rich land of Saskatchewan and Alberta has been drilled, even on a modest scale, for minerals. Working with the law of averages and the still meagre figures on the rates of return, geologists of large experience and only moderate optimism can almost prove that the two provinces will ultimately produce more oil than Oklahoma and California and as much uranium as the rest of the world put together. Conversely, hardly anyone is brave enough to try proving a thing about the future of wheat, except that, as always, it is reasonably hopeful and unreasonably unsure.

Perhaps Bob Pegg, who once quit the prairie in despair and returned to it with confidence, is as good a witness on these matters as anyone. We turned left at the river to pick up his and Betty Pegg's three children, who had been visiting their grandparents. The river was still and white under a foot of snow. I said I hoped that in the summers Bob's children would have as much fun beside the river as he and I and our brothers and sisters once used to have there.

"Oh, they'll like this country," Bob said. "They like it already." After a moment he added, "I wonder if they'll ever really get to know it."

SUPPOSE HERBERT NORMAN *Had* BEEN A COMMUNIST?

(May 11, 1957)

The brutal tragedy of Herbert Norman was far more than a passing incident in human affairs. If we are capable of measuring its full significance it should – and indeed it must – mark the end of a whole era.

Norman was a senior Canadian diplomat. He killed himself after an investigating committee of the United States government repeatedly, and without any evidence that would be admitted in a court of law, insisted on proclaiming to the press and public that he once had been a Communist.

Norman always denied the charge and his denials, after examination of the evidence, were supported by the Canadian government. There is every reason to believe these denials. There is no reason to believe the accusations that they followed. But if we are to realize the full meaning and challenge of this good man's terrible death, we must go a long step further.

Suppose Herbert Norman had been a Communist. Suppose he once did lean toward communism's seductive miasma, as hundreds of thousands of otherwise sensible people did in the half-mad 1920's and the hungry 1930's. Suppose he did hesitate, like so many who once were young and foolish, beneath the moonbeams of Marx and Lenin. Suppose he even reached for those moonbeams before he discovered how apt they are to drift away or thicken into ordinary dust.

Would this have been a fitting reason to hound him to his death? Would this have put real right or justice on the side of the perpetually correct and perpetually careful men who helped to take away his life?

Is there never, we must ask in the name of Herbert Norman, to be an end to the savagery and ignorance of the Robert Morrises? Is there never to be an end to the willingness of people in the highest places to endure them?

The venom of these professional vigilantes and denouncers is appalling enough; their ignorance is far, far worse and far, far more dangerous. They pass final and fatal judgments – usually without anything so inconvenient as a resort to law – on anyone they choose to notice. And the ultimate measure of their folly and irresponsibility is this: Though they elect to be the arbiters of the twentieth century they have not troubled to learn about the twentieth century.

It has been a desperate and confused century, full of poverty and wild prosperity and war. And for its first four decades anyone in North America who did not like the look of it had almost nowhere to turn in the seeking of a political change. In the United

States he could choose between voting Republican or voting Democrat. In Canada he could choose between the Conservatives and the Liberals. But fundamentally he always had to go on voting the same ticket – for a society governed almost wholly by the uncontrolled profit motive, by the law of survival of the fittest.

Is it any wonder that troubled men and women, lacking any other alternative, often turned toward doctrinaire socialism and communism? Fortunately for us all the main attitudes and habits of our society have changed, and greatly for the better. And nearly all the young men and young women of the 1920's and 1930's who once saw communism as the only or the best alternative now believe it was a bad alternative which has long since outlived its dubious usefulness.

This simplest and most apparent political fact of the twentieth century is not within the comprehension of the Robert Morrises, the Joseph McCarthys and those who comfort and support them.

Let these men continue, if they must, in animal ignorance of their own times. But let the rest of us, in the name of humanity and ordinary sense, dismiss them from our councils.

Let us stop asking men of good will and good record to say publicly whether they once were Communists. Stop for the simple reason that if he stays within the law and holds to decent standards of behaviour and utterance, every human individual is entitled to develop, progress or retrogress as an individual within whatever frame of privacy he chooses for himself. We do not hold public interrogations of fly fisherman to discover whether once they fished with worms. We do not call good grey doctors to the witness stand to demand whether they once dreamed of growing up to be cowboys or train robbers. We do not insist that Liberals say whether they once were Conservatives or Republicans whether they once were Democrats. We do not ask respectable and law-abiding matrons to confess before public, quasi-legal bodies whether they ever danced the Charleston or cut out pictures of Rudolph Valentino.

Let me make right now a personal confession which in my mind is not much more important than the confession that I used to smoke cigarettes of dried leaves behind the family garage.

Once I voted Communist.

It was about a quarter of a century ago, when I was even more uneducated than I am today. It was the first vote I ever cast in my life. It was the last Communist vote I ever cast and the last one I expect to cast, and I do not mention the matter through any conscious wish to boast or apologize or make my peace with anyone. I mention it only because it is a fact that is relevant to this discussion.

The Depression was just nicely underway. I was working as a young reporter in Winnipeg at something like twenty dollars a week. The salary was more than adequate for my needs and it may well have been quite a bit more than I was worth. I loved the job, my newspaper and the people I worked with. I did not know a single live Communist and had no special interest in meeting one. No Communist showed any special interest in meeting me.

Yet, in that Manitoba provincial election, I saw what seemed to be due cause to vote for a Communist candidate. For all my own sense of well-being and good fortune, there was not a day when I walked to the office without meeting a dozen panhandlers. Many of the young men I had grown up with were still back home in Saskatchewan out of work or teaching school for thirty dollars a month. Half the families I knew were on relief and the relief rations were desperately small.

The scale of relief and the level of employment, quite clearly, were not going to improve or worsen whether the new provincial government was Grit or Tory. So I voted for a change; any change, the only change in sight. I voted Communist. And, ridiculously enough, so many other befuddled and misguided young persons voted Communist that a Communist was elected to the Manitoba legislature.

There must be several thousand other now considerably older, fleshier and far, far more respectable persons who voted the same way I did on that faraway day. That they did and whether they did is their own private business. It is none of the business of any public investigator, in Washington or Ottawa or anywhere else.

I had not intended to make my own part in the matter public; not because I am especially ashamed of it but because I think it's rather trivial. Its only significance lies in whatever light it may cast on chancy evolution of an average, and therefore chancy, person's politics. Its only meaning – but surely it is a meaning – is that, although some people never overcome their natural tendencies to error, the shape and direction of their errors sometimes change quite remarkably.

We do well to make sure now that Communists do not hold office in policy-making government agencies. The last two decades have cast enough light, enough hard and visible evidence, on the real nature and intent of communism that no one who can see or read or hear need be deceived by it. The Party Communist of today knows exactly what he's doing and exactly what he stands for. He bears small relation to the hopeful, over-trusting idealist of the twenties and the thirties. The insistence of the Morrises and the McCarthys that he is one and the same man betrays more than mere vindictiveness. It betrays stupidity, a simple lack of discernment, a willful closing of the mind to clear essential facts.

But it is not by any means the exclusive fault of a narrow and ignorant few that Herbert Norman was driven to his death. It is a fault of the times and if we wish, we can learn from it.

If we are willing to pay it heed, the tragedy of Herbert Norman can teach us this; to be, above all, wary of the professional investigator and the hired sensation-seeker. To make them both say what they have to say within the law and answer for it, if required, to the law. To make only such accusations against public men as are relevant to the good conduct of the affairs of today; to make them only on evidence, and if they are refuted, to desist from repeating them.

If this alone can be learned from the death of Herbert Norman he will have the epitaph he deserves.

IN DEFENCE OF NATIONALISM

(November 7, 1959)

When Maurice Duplessis died, a whole generation of liberal-minded, anti-segregationist Canadians sighed with relief and hope. It was too bad about Duplessis himself, a man of vast strengths along with his vast failings. But the province he loved, cajoled, ruled and bullied for twenty years was certain to be better off. So was the Dominion he held at arm's length from his province. The Duplessis brand of nationalism was sure to die soon after its leading advocate. That's what large numbers of small-1 liberals were saying on the day Duplessis died.

All of what they were saying may be so. Perhaps it will be to the ultimate advantage of Quebec and Canada if it so turns out to be. But let's not start betting on it. Above all let us not fall into the error of believing that Duplessis's kind of nationalism is a spent and altogether useless force.

122

Nationalism, for better or for worse, is one of the great feeders of our political and military history. In a confused and dangerous world it is one of the few defences left for minorities. It is also one of the commonest excuses for strong-armed majorities. In the aggregate it is a more powerful influence on man's affairs than Communism, Christianity and Democracy combined.

On the debit side nationalism is the force that has set the allegedly peaceful people of Asia at each other's throats – the Indians against the Pakistani, the Chinese against the Indians, half of Latin America against the other half, the Algerians against the French, the Russians against nearly everybody, the Egyptians against the Jews, the people of Canada – thank Heaven in a more limited and less passionate way – against the people of the United States. It can be claimed that what all these antagonists are partly antagonistic about is politics, but it cannot be denied that what they're wholly antagonistic about is boundaries, land, race and, in short, nationalism. On the credit side it can be claimed that millions of people have survived and grown only because they had boundaries to protect them.

To wring our hands, and only wring our hands, over the evils of nationalism will accomplish as little as we have accomplished by wringing our hands over sex and alcohol. A much greater man than Maurice Duplessis once put the case for nationalism better than Duplessis ever did. The person who speaks is Henri Bourassa, just before the First World War: "What I would wish is that between the old English frigate about to sink and the American corsair preparing to pick up the wreckage we should manoeuvre our barque with prudence and firmness, so that it will not be swallowed up in the vortex of one nor be carried away in the wake of the other. Let us not sever the chain too soon, but let us not rivet the links too closely."

Bourassa – like Duplessis but in an infinitely grander style – was a nationalist on two levels. He sought to isolate Canada from the dangerous and disreputable turmoils of the outside world. He also sought to isolate Quebec from the romantic, bloody and, in his eyes, often foolish affairs of Canada.

Bourassa, the parliamentarian, the editor and the orator, understood nearly everything about Canada, and he understood it in both languages. He came along at a propitious time for a real fire-eating nationalist, a time when hundreds of thousands of Canadians who detested everything Bourassa stood for – detested his race, his religion and his politics – were arriving at conclusions

123

similar to his for reasons not quite the same as his. Quite clearly Canada was being hemmed in and suffocated by its two rich relations. One of them, the English relation, was obviously a silly ass. The other rich relation was quite a bit smarter, but he was every bit as objectionable. He talked at the top of his lungs and spilled ashes on the rug. Bourassa kept urging us to get rid of both these benevolent kinfolk, but not to do it too soon.

In 1911 Bourassa and the rest of the country had an almost unparalleled chance to choose up sides. There was a general election coming up. The Prime Minister, Sir Wilfrid Laurier, had just brought off one of the finest strokes of business ever achieved by a Canadian prime minister. He had arranged a tariff treaty with the United States under which Canadian raw materials were to be admitted to the United States almost duty free and their manufactured goods were to come into Canada under about the same conditions. Theoretically this was almost too good to be true. Canada had been seeking something of the sort for more than fifteen years. But the United States had constantly refused to consent. In each of the years 1896, 1900, 1904 and 1908 there had been a general election in each country. In each of those years Canada had voted for lower tariffs and the United States had voted for higher tariffs.

But now Laurier had broken the log jam. He drafted his reciprocity treaty with President William Howard Taft and brought home this fat and long-desired plum with confidence and pride and offered it to his presumably grateful people. What happened? The people began asking what that damned scheming Yankee scoundrel Taft was up to now. They burned Taft in effigy and went roaring through the streets singing rude songs about him. Laurier's Tory opponents, who at first had thought they were altogether undone by Laurier's brilliant statesmanship, plucked up their courage and rushed to the attack. They dusted off old battle cries from the days of the sacred John A. Macdonald – "No truck or trade with the Yankees", "A British subject I was born: a British subject I will die." The railway baron, William Van Horne, took a horrified look at reciprocity and cried aloud that he was "out to bust the damned thing." And he and his fellow protectionists got a great deal of unintentional help from their opponents – and opposing nationalists – in the United States. Champ Clark, the speaker of the United States House of Representatives, proclaimed, "I hope to see the day when the American flag will float over every square foot of the British North American possession clear to the north pole." A U.S. Senator was heard to announce, "Canadian annexation is the logical conclusion of reciprocity with Canada." President Taft himself announced solemnly, "Canada is at the parting of the ways."

All this was good red raw meat to the Canadian protectionists, who rushed up their reserves. Rudyard Kipling himself cabled on the eve of the election, "It is her soul that Canada risks today." A group of Montreal clubwomen passed a resolution saying that reciprocity meant "Annexation, injury to home life and the marriage tie, a lessening of national religion, morals and patriotism."

On the eve of the election the harassed and hopelessly misunderstood Laurier found himself crying forth his own epitaph; "I am branded in Quebec as a traitor to the French and in Ontario as a traitor to the English. In Quebec I am branded as a Jingo and in Ontario as a Separatist. In Quebec I am attacked as an Imperialist and in Ontario as an anti-Imperialist."

When election day came Laurier and the reciprocity treaty were snowed under. But history has almost forgotten that Laurier's successor, Sir Robert Borden, was a nationalist too.

Very soon Borden's new government, which had gone into power on a surge of nationalism, was forced to defend itself against charges of colonialism. And now the foreign devil that Canadians began eyeing with suspicion and alarm was not the kindly Mr. Taft but a brash young Englishman named Winston Churchill. Churchill was the First Lord of the Admiralty in Britain and he was telling Canada how to build and run its navy. Or rather how not to build and run it. Everybody knew there was going to be a war with Germany; Churchill said Canada should send over men, ships and guns but not try to manage them herself. This put the young Englishman right at the eye of a fresh cyclone. One maddened Canadian Member of Parliament got up in the House of Commons, read the American Declaration of Independence, then read one of Winston Churchill's patronizing memoranda to the Canadian government, and choked forth, "That document is calculated to cause more irritation to undermine more seriously our constitutional freedom than any document that has come from authority in Great Britain to any colony since the days of Lord North." Another M.P. prophesied that Churchill had taken "the first step in the direction that will ultimately mean the separation of the Dominion from the . . . Empire."

As an advocate of protection, it was not surprising that during the 1911 election Borden had allowed his supporters to use anti-American verses like this:

Lord God of our fathers, rise up at
Thy people's cry
For blindness has stricken the nation
and the doom of our land grows
nigh.
Rise, rise up ere it falls, Lord, and
blast with the fire of Thy mouth
The treason that barters our birth-
right for the gold of the Kings of
the South.

Borden's suspicion of the United States was quite in character with his personal background and his political tradition. His
suspicion of the United Kingdom was less well known. As a Tory
and an Imperialist Borden should have been, in theory, an uncriti-
cal supporter of the British government, but he wasn't. After he
was elected and the British Cabinet refused to give him information or consult him about what was going on during the war he
sent the Cabinet this message:

It can hardly be expected that we shall put 400,000 or 500,-
000 men in the field and willingly accept the position of having no
more voice and receiving no more consideration than if we were
toy automata. Any person cherishing such an expectation har-
bours an unfortunate and even dangerous delusion. Is this war
being waged by the United Kingdom alone, or is it a war being
waged by the whole Empire? If I am correct in supposing that the
second hypothesis must be accepted, then why do the statesmen of
the British Isles arrogate to themselves solely the methods by
which it shall be carried on. . . . It is for them to suggest the
method. . . . If there is no available method and if we are expected
to continue in the role of automata, the whole situation must be
reconsidered. . . . Procrastination, indecision, inertia, doubt and
hesitation and many other undesirable qualities have made themselves felt in this war.

This was the voice of a nationalist. Mackenzie King echoed
it much later:

Anything like a direct or indirect attempt at Downing Street
to tell the people of the Dominions what they should do is certain
to prove just as injurious to so-called "Imperial solidarity" as any
attempt at interference in matters of purely domestic concern. If
membership within the British Empire means participation by the
Dominion in any and every war in which Great Britain becomes

involved, without consultation, conference or agreement of any kind, I can see no hope for an enduring relationship.

It is not altogether a coincidence that the least successful Prime Minister of this century, Arthur Meighen, seemed to many Canadians – although the estimate was grossly unfair – to be more an Englishman than a Canadian. It is not altogether a coincidence that John Diefenbaker, many years later, spoke up loudly for nationalism while Lester Pearson spoke up quietly for internationalism and that Diefenbaker became our Prime Minister and Pearson didn't.

What I am contending is that the opponents of nationalism – of whom this writer is one by instinct but not by practice – are enormously right and, alas, half blind. Call nationalism what you will – the herd instinct, the group instinct, the instinct to form ranks behind barriers of geography, history, race, colour or religion – it is still there and it is still almost irresistible. We do well in hoping it will go away, along with our other dangerous habits. But we'll achieve nothing by assuming it has gone away already or is on the way to going away. To lick it would be admirable; the next best thing is to join it.

In Asia, in Europe, in Africa, in North America, in Canada and – to return to the original point – in Quebec, nationalism will not die overnight. Quebec nationalism will not die with Maurice Duplessis any more than Canadian nationalism died with King, Russian nationalism with Stalin or English nationalism with Victoria. And minorities in general, whatever their origin or location, are most unlikely – and perhaps even unwise – to abandon their nationalism until majorities abandon theirs. That time is a long time away and the more clearly we recognize the fact the fewer misunderstandings there'll be within the universal anarchy of nations, states and provinces.

A REPORTER AT LARGE AMONG THE CONGOLESE

(June 17, 1961)

It comes as a terrible humiliation for an old war correspondent to admit that covering the military campaigns of twenty years ago may not, after all, have been the most complicated and exacting journalistic assignment of his time.

After a month in the Congo and, thus far, very brief stops in half a dozen other African countries, I must confess to a foolish yearning for the simplicity and order of the beaches of Normandy, the polders of Holland and the mountains and river gorges of Italy. In those times and places, it is true, you stood a much better chance of losing your life, but in these ones you stand a much better chance of losing your mind. The frustrations and contradictions and above all the uncertainties and red tape and the delays used to be lumped under the single word snafu. Now the word that embraces them all is Congo. As a connoisseur of relative potencies I would rate Congo about ninety overproof compared to ninety underproof for snafu.

In the old, real war, when two men started shooting at each other at least one of them had some idea why. Not so now. In those days there were maps to show who the enemy was and there was similar information available about your friends. Not so now. There are at least nine main and three hundred minor tribal groups in the Congo, and there are roughly as many languages and dialects. This being the kind of world it is – all over and not only in the Congo – it has become the thing to start throwing spears, rocks, bombs or anything else handy at anybody you don't understand or recognize. In the Congo and in most of the rest of Africa people have been living a long time and almost unbearably on the edge of suspicion and fear. A man like me whose visible credentials are freckles and a Stetson hat should really not expect, perhaps, to fade unnoticed into the mud villages of the Gombe, Bwaka and Mongo tribes. Therefore I forgive, without reservation, the fifty Gombe tribesmen who chased me (they on foot and I in a truck) out of a village between Libenge and Yakoma near the equator.

The tribal and racial hazards endemic here are, however, very minor compared to the administrative ones. It is hard to conceive that a botanical and zoological wilderness so vast as this could be surpassed by a parallel bureaucratic wilderness, but that is one of the things happening in the Congo. The Belgians pulled out in June and July 1960, leaving the Congolese with a total of seventeen university graduates and a handful of other *évolués,* bright young men, eager young men and willing young men charged at an instant's notice with reorganizing and administering a nation a quarter as large as Canada in area and more than two thirds as large in population. Even without the tribal wars and the political wars out here and the additional propaganda wars in the great underbrush of the United Nations in New York, their task would be very close to hopeless. Just the same many of them do try, and try astonishingly well.

I have met a number of these young New Africans. The most impressive of them is thirty-year-old Albert N'dele, president of the national bank in the national capital of Léopoldville. He has the lithe good looks of a Sugar Ray Robinson or a Harry Belafonte, an excellent mind and an almost saintly determination to forgive the sins of the past and forget the crimes done in the name of colour.

There seemed, nevertheless, a certain fatal symbolism in the contrast between him and his surroundings. His office is on the second floor of the Central Bank Building, really a square balcony looking down a well into rows of desks and cages. All around the balcony and at the desks and cages below, his young assistants were toiling under slow, paddle-bladed electric fans to pin the country's drifting fiscal hulk to some sort of anchor. (In any saloon uptown it was still impossible for a white visitor to buy a drink without first being importuned by the bartender to sell him American dollars, pegged by the bank at fifty francs, for anything up to eighty-five or ninety.)

Outside N'dele's private office, his young secretary examined my passport, my vaccination certificate, my air travel card and my local *laissez-passer* and then directed me to fill out another form explaining the reason for my visit. Then he explained that the president could not possibly receive visitors as he was with one of his key supervisors. After a further wait I explained again that I really did have a firm and explicit appointment and asked the secretary if he would please make sure that Monsieur was actually and in fact engaged. With an amiable shrug, the secretary got up, went to the door, bent down and looked through the keyhole and then escorted me into a room in which the only occupant, besides Mr. N'dele, was a man who was trying and persistently failing to hang a curtain and who continued to try and fail throughout our interview.

It was only by accident, a week or so later, that I discovered the meaning of N'dele's name in Lingala, the regional lingua franca. N'dele means two things: the day before yesterday, and the day after tomorrow. If ever a man and his country were confronted simultaneously with the burdens of both those days they are Albert N'dele and the Congo.

Like all other transients here I have to admit that my own transient little troubles have occupied me far too much. These include such rudimentary things as the staggering heat in the tropical bush as well as the lurking python and the deadly tsetse fly, all of which up to now I had believed to be the melodramatic inventions of the men I used to read in *Chums* and the *Boy's Own Annual.*

One night I woke up in a steamy ranch house three hundred miles in the bush beyond the last U.N. frontier of Coquilhatville. Drums were beating in the valley below, exactly as the *Boy's Own Annual* of 1922. Less than five months ago human flesh had been on sale like beef in the public market of the village of Bongobo, twenty miles away. (This is one of those silly, too-pat romances that visiting reporters grab at too eagerly; but I checked it specifically and independently with the Belgian former chief administrator and judge of the district, with two Canadian doctors, with a Belgian doctor, with three Congolese *évolués,* with a Belgian nun and a Belgian priest, with a Portuguese white hunter and a Lolita-type Gombe bar-girl. They all said the stories of open, commercialized cannibalism were true; three claimed to have seen the evidence for themselves and they all wondered why it should be doubted.)

Anyway, the drums woke me up and I hollered insouciantly through the moonlit doorway to my host, René Borrey, *"Qu'est-ce qui se passe là-bas, monsieur? On fait beaucoup de bruit."*

"Dormez," Borrey suggested politely. "In the morning we'll have time to find out what's going on."

In the morning we found out that a few Gombe hunters had moved into the corrals, speared two of Borrey's little Kohomae cattle, hacked out the choice cuts and left the rest behind. The economic loss was not serious, but to Borrey the spiritual loss was like another of many hammer blows. *"Avant,"* he said, "this could not have happned. *En ces temps* it would have been incredible." *Avant* does not need an object here; when you speak of *ces temps* everyone knows what times are spoken of. Before the flight of the Belgians, before the liberation, in the time of the old regime. . . .

"Perhaps at last they'll drive me out," Borrey said sorrowfully. The day before, at their home a hundred and fifty kilometres away, I had met his charming mulatto wife and their quadroon daughter, Hilda. "I have been here thirteen years and they have been here all their lives. If I could be sure Belgium would treat them as kindly as the Congo has treated me. . . . I just don't know what we'll do or when."

That conclusion – "I just don't know . . ." – comes crashing in everywhere with stunning weight. "We're down to six knives and six forks," a well-to-do businessman in Katanga told me. "We've got five bedrooms in our house but only six spoons. When we got the first outbursts after liberation I packed my wife in the car and we ran south into Rhodesia. Then I came back and discovered to my amazement that everything was still there. But since then I've been shipping our belongings gradually to Belgium; we're not really living here any more, we're just camping out. I'd like to stay about fifteen years but I'm ready to move in fifteen minutes and when we do go that's how fast we'll go."

One dark night in the fragrant-flowered city of Elisabethville I was looking for the British consulate and ran into a couple of other campers-out. They were a two-man patrol of young Irishmen from the sorely beleaguered and greatly detested United Nations force. "My God in Heaven, man," the twenty-one-year-old corporal said as we parted, "don't ask me what I'm doin' here. If I ever get back to Dublin they'll have to put me in one of them rocket things to get me out again."

I had a good, if wary, talk the next day with three officers of Moise Tshombe's Foreign Legion. Since they have been officially condemned and ordered to get out by the United Nations Security Council, Tshombe's mercenaries are under instructions to pretend they don't exist, at least until their boss wins or gives up the key struggle for the Congo's wealth and power. But in Tshombe's rich, crucial province of Katanga they are visible everywhere, in their bush hats, red epaulets, camouflage jackets and desert boots. Some of their Belgian predecessors have heeded their country's and the UN's order to go home, but some have just refused and Tshombe's tough army is still well led by Europeans, white Africans and Englishmen. Of the three officers I persuaded to talk to me (on the condition that I wouldn't ask or try to find out their names), one was from South Africa, one was a white hunter from Kenya and the third was a recent public-school graduate just out from England. Two of the three wore all the standard badges of service in the Eighth Army and one of them had the Military Cross. The ribbons weren't needed to prove they were hard and experienced.

"Will we fight?" the senior one repeated in reply to my question. "Of course we will. That's what we're paid for, and the pay is good and it comes on time."

How did they expect to make out in the event of a show-down? "Well," the senior officer said, "we've already licked the northern tribes. We can lick them again. We can lick the Léopold army and the Orientale army, any combination of them."

What about the United Nations troops? "Well, I hope it doesn't come to that. These Irishmen are very good. They're good people and good soldiers and it'd be no fun to tangle with them. Besides, if they use their planes to reinforce. . . ."

Out at the Elisabethville airport the tough, bewildered young UN Irishmen were still marching with fixed bayonets and practising their native game of hurling in the little tented camp near by. Tshombe's tough old soldiers of fortune from the old armies of the desert were still striding past them, with their bush hats riding low and their faded hunters' eyes careful and alert.

For a person travelling on the edges of the explosion – not just the explosion of the Congo but perhaps of most of Africa – it becomes imperative, now and then, to pause and ask if there's anything really to take heart in.

Likely not. But you can pick up an occasional lesson if you listen carefully. The most useful one I have had came from Gustavo Duran, who for five months headed the trickiest and most dangerous of all the United Nations missions, in Orientale province and on the raging frontier between the homicidal Balubas and Luluas. In the Spanish Civil War, Duran was the youngest general on the Loyalist side. There he lost magnificently, and perhaps time will prove he's lost again here.

The advice he gave me, as he went out and I went in through Léopoldville, was this: "Play the place by ear. Don't expect anybody to do the expected. Don't do the expected thing yourself."

He was thinking partly of the negotiations he'd conducted to save the lives of eight Belgian paratroopers who were captured and brought to Stanleyville in the first main wave of trouble. Their execution looked like a matter of hours and Duran hurried to intercede with Major-General Victor Lundula, the local commander-in-chief. At first he seemed to be getting nowhere.

"Then," he said, "I decided to be devious and Congolese. 'These men are in the wrong,' I told the general. 'They have done a very bad thing. But they meant no harm to any person here. They were only trying to protect their own people.'

"Now," Duran went on, "I played my trump card. 'Besides,' I said, 'their lives are worth nothing to you. You are fully entitled to impose a heavy fine on them – a very heavy fine. Fine them ten million francs, twenty million francs, and their government will have no choice but to pay.'

"I thought that would do it," Duran continued, "and it did do it, but in a different way than I had imagined. Instead of grabbing at the bribe, Lundula looked me in the eye and said: 'We do not barter lives for money. If we spare these men they will go free absolutely and no money will change hands.' By being devious and Congolese, against my better nature, I had unwittingly forced Lundula to be noble and Spanish against his worst nature."

Duran's injunction to play things here by ear stood me in good stead one loud and moonlit night when I was riding a train through the High Katanga. I was on the way to see the fabulous copper and cobalt mines of Union Minière near Kolwezi and the only way to get there was to get aboard one of the few trains still running, pay your fare and hope for the best.

Up to about 2 A.M. the best was not too bad. The ancient Souris-to-Oxbow type train was groaning and lurching to a halt at every grass-thatched whistlestop, but the giant anthills and the moonlit palm trees waved us gently on. I'd had a pleasant good-night chat with the other occupant of the sleeping compartment, a young Basanga clerk, and we were both at last on the verge of some much-needed sleep. Then, in an instant, the whole place was in an African uproar. A lady the size of Man Mountain Dean was glowering above my berth, shouting that it belonged to her and the two well-fed children right behind her. The conductor, who already had my ticket but pretended he hadn't, was behind the children. Behind him, as there always is, anywhere, any time, and for any reason, there stood a Congolese soldier waving a gun.

Remembering Duran's advice, I called on my few words of Lingala, Luba and Tshoko and my pidgin French and delivered the following ultimatum: "Ladies and gentlemen, I don't care how many people sleep in this berth tonight, but I'm going to be one of them." With that they clattered grumpily down the corridor and, as I discovered in the morning, dispossessed a minor official of the civil service.

As I started out to say, it's not exactly like Bernières-sur-Mer, the Falaise Gap or the Breskens Point, but it's every bit as memorable.

(June 16, 1962)

One of the most important questions about the changing state of our nation can be asked in one short and, to some, disturbing question: "What has happened to the fishing?"

It used to be taken as a matter of course that anybody from anywhere, no matter how incompetent, no matter how unfamiliar with the ways of fish, could go fishing anywhere in Canada and long before he was at the bottom of the first jug of rye he'd have a boatful of rainbow trout, cut-throat trout, speckled trout, lake trout, Arctic char, Arctic grayling, mudpuds, ling, pike, doré, perch, sturgeon, small-mouth bass, large-mouth bass, silver bass, Atlantic salmon, Tyee salmon, landlocked salmon, tommycod, herring, whitefish, smelt, blue-gills, rock bass, sunfish or pumpkinseeds and occasionally a medium-sized white whale.

Fishing has been (and still is, according to the tourist agents), our most dependable national treasure. All you had to do, according to the lost and lovely myth, was wet a line anywhere between Corner Brook, Newfoundland, and Port Alberni, British Columbia, and the fish would come to you so thick and fast and big and splendid that you were lucky to get away with your life. It was never wholly true, of course, not even in the days when the whole population consisted of Hurons, Iroquois, moose and great golden pickerel. But at least three million people still go fishing in Canada every year. They spend nearly ten million dollars on fishing licenses alone, even though in some provinces, including Ontario, the residents don't need licenses. No one can offer any sensible estimate of how much more they spend on food, lodging, tackle, gasoline and the wine of the country.

Other North Americans rush across our borders by the tens of thousands, full of towering dreams. Those of us who are more or less indigenous are equally optimistic. We race happily from Collingwood, Ontario, to Three Rivers, Quebec (or just as likely the other way around), or from North Battleford, Saskatchewan, to Jasper Park, Alberta (and again the other way around), in the undying belief that the place we're going to is The Right Place, the place where the lunkers lie waiting and hungry.

The disillusioning facts are that (a) the lunkers probably aren't there in the first place and (b) if they are, they're much too sophisticated to be caught by the first stray dude from Peoria or Westmount. For the average fisherman it has become extremely difficult to catch fish of any size or in any numbers in the Fisherman's Paradise of Canada. A really great fisherman – and there probably aren't more than two dozen of these in the whole world – will somehow catch fish anywhere. A rich fisherman, a man who can charter a plane, is still almost certain to get great fish in any province of the Dominion. This usually involves going north as far as the waters that feed Hudson Bay and the Arctic. There's some magnificent salmon water further south, mainly in the Maritimes. But a great deal of the good water in the Maritimes has been sold or leased to private interests and if you want to fish it you must either pay a huge fee or risk being arrested as a poacher. There are a few good streams and lakes in the accessible parts of British Columbia and Alberta and there are some man-killing muskellunge in the St. Lawrence, within a short bus ride of Montreal. But these aren't fish that the man from Peoria or Westmount ever sees. According to biologists, fish were on this planet well ahead of men and according to many political thinkers they may be here long after man has left. They are down there outsmarting us, and the closer they are to the haunts and habitations of man the craftier they get.

This sounds like a mournful view of the prospects of the angler in Canada but it's not meant to be. Catching fish is surely only one of the pleasures of fishing and fishing is still, all over Canada, a source of huge and varied pleasure. There are birds around, trees around, flowers around and occasionally even a willing fish around.

This note on fishing will not deal with the Never-Never-Lands, the places so hard to reach that the casual week-end fisherman has no chance of getting there. It's addressed to the man who says, four or five times a year, "Say, Clarisse," or "Say Bertha, what would you say if I went fishing with old George and Charlie for maybe next Saturday and Sunday?"

If this man is looking primarily for fish, he should buy them at the store and stay home. If, however, he's caught some intimation of the true meaning of fishing he should kiss Clarisse or Bertha good-bye and get moving. The essence of his quest is the quest itself.

One of the finest two or three writers on fishing, one whose quiet knowledge of his subject and quiet command of his language have earned him a reputation all over the world, is the Vancouver Island author and magistrate, Roderick Haig-Brown. When I asked him if he'd tell me where he looked for the best fishing of all he answered, "The best for me, as it is to all fly enthusiasts, is in the nearest stream that holds worthwhile fish. This is where we know the standards and can test our performances against our own past performances. It is full of recognitions and echoes and other delights. It may not be good fishing in the regulation sense, but it is bound to be the best."

Gregory Clark, an equally famous and eloquent fisherman, refuses flatly to admit that there are any bad places to fish, any bad books on fishing or any bad stories about fishing. "In that realm," he says, "criticism does not enter."

No two people have exactly the same thoughts and emotions about fishing. No two have the same ideas and visions about the best places to go. Talking still about the spots close to the places where Clarisse and Bertha will allow their menfolk briefly off the leash, there are at least two outstanding lakes left in Canada. One of these is Memphremagog, in the Eastern Townships of Quebec, where anybody is almost sure, at the worst, of a good catch of perch and anybody who's lucky could run into good small-mouth bass or lake trout or even the wild and beautiful landlocked salmon.

The second great lake for quick-week-end, city fishermen is without doubt Lake Simcoe in Ontario. Lake Simcoe is an amazing stretch of water, its south end only forty miles from Toronto and therefore within an hours's drive of more than two million people. It's got small-mouth bass – and no one interested in fishing should never forget that with the possible exception of the salt-water tarpon, the salt-water bonefish and the slab-sided, side-winding African pompano, the small-mouth is the toughest fighting fish there is. (There will be cries of outrage from defenders of the muskie, the steelhead trout and the Atlantic salmon, but the thing to remember is that these other fish outweigh the gallant bass by two, four or six to one. Imagine tying into a twenty-five-pound small-mouth! It's enough to scare a man out of a year's growth.)

There are many other fish in Lake Simcoe besides the marvelous small-mouth – pike, whitefish, herring, perch, catfish, an occasional rainbow trout and an astounding number of lake trout, as clean and tough as nails, weighing anywhere from two to twenty pounds can be found.

Saskatchewan is the only province where it's almost impossible to get good fishing without traveling a long way from the urban areas. If you go north you'll be in reach of magnificent lake trout, grayling and pike. In the inhabited parts it's different. I grew up in the south-east, non-fishing part of Saskatchewan, right on the border of North Dakota. Every spring we'd go to the C.P.R. dam below our town. We'd half-swim and half-climb up to the dam and grab fat suckers out by hand and then take them up-town to sell to the owner of the Chinese laundry or the owner of the Chinese café. (The café owner couldn't resell them to his customers but he claimed that he, personally, found them delicious.)

Later in the year there would be big mud turtles dozing the rocks below the dam and in due course the laundryman or the café owner would acquire them too. A purist might deny that this was fishing at all. In the most heroic and noble sense it may not have been. But after many years of trial and error, defeat and a very occasional victory, I have arrived at the unalterable conclusion that anything that seems like fishing is fishing.

In Manitoba, leaving aside a few semi-secret places, it's also necessary to go a long way north to get what most people define as good fishing. It's easier in Alberta where you start right on the main highways to hit the foothills and the Rockies and the fast water. Once, I was visiting my brother-in-law Phil Austin at his ranch near Cochrane, less than forty miles from Calgary. There was a little stream below his house, roiled from a recent rain and hardly ten feet wide. At daybreak I went out to the garden and found a few worms (those who object to bait fishing may return the magazine and have their money refunded.) I borrowed a fly-rod and went sheepishily, expecting nothing in the way of fish, to the little stream to get some of the lovely morning air. At once I was assaulted by a horde of cut-throat and rainbow trout the like of which I'll never see again. I took back a dozen for breakfast, good-sized ones for that kind of water, up to fifteen inches.

In Ontario I've run into the same sort of astonishment only once. It was on a little creek near a place called Campbellford. For years Andy Anderson and I made a practice of buying inch-to-the-mile maps. Then we'd identify a stream where there would or should be trout and we'd start map-reading, moving back and forth along the cross-roads until we hit a place where the water looked promising and the No Trespassing signs were either non-existent or so eroded we could pretend not to have seen them.

By this process we arrived at the creek near Campbellford on a bright Sunday morning and fought our way through brush and swamp. Andy politely stayed a little behind while I floundered on until I found a place where I was able to keep the back cast clear of the trees and still hit the little strip of water with the forward cast. I thought I'd reached a chub hole and was ready to move on the instant the first chub – usually considered a trash fish – made its appearance. Instead, and I'd bet my life it could not possibly happen again, fifteen gleaming speckled trout came out of that one little pool before I moved my feet. Not one was over twelve inches long but not a single one was under ten. These statistics are meaningless to anyone who hasn't tried fishing close to the city streets of Canada; to anyone who has tried they will be as unbelievable as they still remain to me.

You just can't generalize any more about fishing in this country. You will get no agreement anywhere although you will still get honest passion everywhere. I brought the matter up with another of my favorite fishing companions, Charles Lynch, a Maritimer who has been lured to Ottawa. "It is my theory," Lynch says, "that few of the inhabitants of the great sporting regions of our land have any sporting instincts, nor do they have the faintest idea of what is meant by same. Their basic thought, I feel sure, is that the sporting fisherman is a sucker and the fly-fisherman is completely demented. Some of them are splendid fly-fishermen themselves, as the result of a lifetime of pretending that this is the way they prefer to fish. But turn your back on them for an instant, or let them go off for some fish on their own and out come the dynamite sticks, the worms and the jigs. I have had too many guides revert to this type on me to believe otherwise – let them detect a streak of scoundrel in their paying guest and by mid-day they will be suggesting that the native way of fishing be tried."

Another friend of mine once made an equally cogent comment on some fishing guides. Bruce West and I were after pickerel and Great Northern pike in Quebec and had been placed at the mercy of a Montagnais guide who kept rowing the boat in circles or in the wrong direction, kept dropping the anchor in fourteen inches of water even though it was the sort of day when any sane fish had to be lying at fourteen feet, and getting things so genially fouled up that you couldn't help suspecting you had somehow been plunged into the middle of an old Laurel and Hardy movie. At last, through some miracle of luck or divination, I managed to get a long spinning cast far enough away from the boat to reach a respectable amount of water and through a further miracle a huge Great Northern grabbed it. I was using a two-pound test line and when, forty minutes later, West and I finally got a look at the fish, we judged it weighed at least twelve. My reel had jammed and so the usual (and revolting) features of the safety clutch or star drag weren't working. When the fish wanted to run, it had to be allowed to run or it would have snapped the line. In the only feat of angling for which I have the slightest right to be remembered I brought the fish up near, let it run, brought it near, let it run; West and I had both decided we must release it anyway because it was a very fine fish and we didn't need it. But through chivalry or vanity I wanted desperately to get it into the net long enough to have a decent look at it and release the hook properly. At last the big and handsome fish did come near enough for boating. Our guide made a lunge for it with the net and succeeded in hitting it on the head and knocking it free. The fish slowly swam away, no more tired than I. "Good heavens," West whispered to me, glancing at our faithful guide. "We got another of those correspondence-school Indians."

Lynch and West have both, of course, pinpointed one of the two inescapable curses of fishing. Next to the fishing guide and perhaps even surpassing him in sheer hideousness is the outboard motor. The outboard motor is one of the three or four most awful contraptions ever invented. For sheer uselessness combined with nuisance value I would rate it about even with the pyramids and the disc jockey. I have especially bad luck with outboard motors, partly because I have bad luck with my fishing companions. Most of them pretend either to be permanently disabled or feebler than I am and one or two come right out and admit they're lazier. Whatever their excuses are, there I am floundering down a cliff or through a jungle of poison ivy carrying a horrible, smelly, malevolent, leaky machine that the manufacturers claim weighs a mere thirty-eight pounds and that anybody fighting it knows to weigh at least a fifth of a ton. I fall down an average of six times, with the shouts of my friends ringing encouragement behind. When I get to the boat and start fixing the motor on it I fall into the water, at a very conservative estimate, twice. My friends are now either dissolved in mirth or solemnly united in offering fresh advice. But through sheer strength of character I get the dreadful device attached. Then it won't work anyway.

Once – it seems a very long time ago – I actually got an outboard motor down the hill, fixed it to the boat and got it going. Almost immediately we hit a rock and broke a shear-pin. While I was putting in a new shear-pin the motor escaped my grasp and plummeted twenty feet to the bottom of the lake. A good place for it.

Fishing of any kind in Canada can involve little misadventures like this, but the pines and birch are still there. In the spring the poplars and aspens greet you like shy young maidens and in the fall the turning oaks and maples fairly shout at you and hold up their colours like medieval warriors.

It is still a good country in which to fish and, whether you catch fish or not, a good country in which to be and look around.

FOURTEEN DAYS IN CYPRUS

(June 20, 1964)

The trick may be in the eye of the viewer but war or the imminence of war can do things physically for a country, as approaching marriage does for a bride. When did the skies and downs of Britain gleam as they gleamed in the years from 1939 through 1942? When did the olive groves and mountain sunsets of Italy beckon as they beckoned in the late summer and autumn of 1943? When did the Norman poppies glow so red as amid the turning wheat and the black death's-head *Achtung! Minen!* signs of 1944?

Spring, it is said, is always the best season in Cyprus. The river-beds are as dry as pavement and the great central plain of the Mesaoria, pillaged of its forest cover by Pharaoh's shipbuilders and gnawed to the bone by a thousand generations of half-wild goats, is gaunt and parched already. But the hillsides are fragrant with cypress, cedars, and stalwart, fodder-bearing carob trees, the new grapes are ripening on the valley slopes and the next sweet oranges will soon be ready, too. The mountain ranges are crowned with castles, abbeys and battlements as old as Richard Coeur de Lion, the sea is indescribably and unbearably blue, the sky is clear and unflawed, the temperature is seventy-four, and there won't be a drop of rain before September. Even the Mediterranean smells of North Africa and Sicily – the wog and Ay-rab smells of Tunis, Algiers and Catania – are miraculously missing. It was off this lustrous coastline that Aphrodite rose from the foam. This is where Adonis came to meet her.

Even for a man still dazzled by the scenery it takes only a few minutes to get a fix on the military situation. My room at the Ledra Palace – one of the four hotels on the island officially classified as deluxe by the government tourist bureau – is a corner room with a balcony, facing the Green (i.e. the front) Line from both exposures. The Turkish section of the old walled city of Nicosia is just beyond the main road and the moat. There is a Turkish pillbox and a line of Turkish trenches 148 counted paces (my count) straight up the road, and there is a Greek fortified house eighty paces down the road the other way. Directly below me on the main floor of the hotel is the entrance to the headquarters of the 26th Medium Regiment, Royal Artillery, now attached to the United Nations Peace-Keeping Force. Directly above on the second floor is the regimental command post.

In the large military anatomy, the island's 115,000 Turkish Cypriots occupy half of walled Nicosia, all of the walled city of Famagusta, and fourteen of the sixteen miles of the main road between Nicosia and the lovely little harbour town of Kyrenia. The 460,000 Greek Cypriots hold Kyrenia itself as well as most of the other cities, towns and villages. For munitions the Turks within the main Green Line-Nicosia-Kyrenia enclave, like those in the refugee towns and villages scattered elsewhere throughout the island, are dependent on the weapons and ammunition they stockpiled in less urgent times, plus the home-made bullets, grease guns and mortars they can make in a few hidden cellars, plus the trickle of NATO hand-me-downs and gun-runners' contraband they are able to smuggle through the Greek blockade. Thanks to the Turkish Red Crescent, operating under what protection it can get from the United Nations and the Red Cross, none of the Turks, even those in the most isolated and hemmed-in villages, are as yet going short of food or medicine. But the logic and the logistics of the situation make it clear that the Turkish Cypriots' only hope of a continuing stalemate, much less a victory, lies beyond the shores of Cyprus.

On this Friday, a particularly quiet day all over the island, the only problem in crossing the check-points and barricades is remembering to drive on the left and shift gears, left-handed, on a rented English Morris. Another hazard is that all the armed men at all the check-points wear the blue serge uniform of the Cypriot civil police. To a stranger a Greek Cypriot looks exactly the same as a Turkish Cypriot – that is to say, rather short, swarthy and fierce, but still, oddly enough, rather friendly. They all, Turk and Greek alike, talk some English and their accents are as hard to separate as their looks. They all carry the same vintage weapons – second-hand American M-1 rifles or British Lee-Enfields or stocky little Stens. Although their larger fortified houses, sandbag breastworks and mountain dugouts sometimes fly the star and crescent of Turkey or the blue and white national flag of Greece, the roadblocks seldom show their colours. Until you get the geographical niceties absolutely straight, it is as well to keep the small talk with the sentries limited and non-committal. In my first drive through the shatteringly beautiful Kyrenia mountains, I passed nine Turkish barricades, none of which held me up longer than it took to open my passport and inspect the photograph. Usually there was a brief exchange of pleasantries – "Quieter today?" or "Good luck," – all neutral enough in the strict sense of the word. But after nine such passages I felt some vague affinity with the Turks and at the tenth roadblock, just south of Kyrenia, I was on the verge of passing on the observation that the damned Greeks were a little less trigger-happy today. Just in time I remembered that according to the map I had just crossed the Green Line again and these were the damned Greeks I was talking to. "The damned – uh – shooting in the pass was slowed down," I reported as a normal courtesy between wayfarers.

An official of the Cyprus Government Information Office invites me to dinner, plies me with excellent red wine out of a wooden cask and a feast of meze – a sort of Olympian smorgasbord that would bring Achilles himself to his knees. The wily Levantine's main purpose, of course, is not so much to stuff me with *sautéed* octopus, dolma, moussaka and halloumi as to stuff me with Greek propaganda. Having already taken a week's cram course in the official literature of both sides. I do my feeble best to fight the case for the absent Turks. Just before we part I put a final for-the-sake-of-argument to my host. "Suppose, suddenly, you were given the absolute right to fix the terms of settlement between Greek Cyprus and Turkish Cyprus. The only stipulation is that you must not annihilate either community or its fundamental human rights and liberties. What would you do?"

"What would I do?" If the smile is meant to be weary and wordly-wise it also contains a great depth of sorrow. "I'd turn the whole thing over to someone else."

Historical Note: In his book, Bitter Lemons, *Lawrence Durrell quotes a Greek Cypriot proverb:*
If the stone falls on the egg, alas for the egg.
If the egg falls on the stone – alas for the egg.

They are never sure, particularly in the mountains, what Saturdays and Sundays will bring. School is out, some of the shops are closed and – largely among the much more numerous Greeks – little groups of boys and men go out for an afternoon's or a weekend's sniping just as, elsewhere, they go out for eighteen holes of golf or an overnight fishing trip.

Today the firing started early on both sides of the road leading up from Nicosia to the mountains, over the height of land and down again to the blue jewel-box harbour of Kyrenia. Standing near Company "C" headquarters of the Canadian Royal 22e Regiment, Canada's main UN contingent, I make a spot-check toward mid-morning – sixty-eight shots in one metred minute. A few come from the direction of St. Hilarion Castle, the anchor of the Turks' position on the west of the road. Most are from the three tall peaks to the east – two of them held by the Turks and one by the Greeks. Nearly all are single shots, probably from bolt-action rifles, but there's a splatter or two of rapid fire that sounds like a Bren. Major Pat Tremblay, whose Canadian soldiers are enjoined by the UN's instructions to create peace without giving orders or taking anybody's gun or bullets away from him, is pretty sure that just before breakfast two mortar bombs lobbed in from St. Hilarion to the Greek village on the reverse slope of the mountain he's christened Gin. Tremblay, a Second World War veteran with a Military Medal from Korea, can't help deploring the waste of ammunition on both sides. Nowhere are the two hill forces less than five hundred yards apart, and in most places the distance is two or three times that great. Probably not one shot in a hundred is aimed at a visible target and not one in a thousand is doing any actual harm. "One thing I know," Tremblay says professionally. "If I was a Greek I'd attack." Further down, on the other side of the pass, a British detachment is watchdogging another long-range exchange in which the Greeks are trying to dislodge the Turks from a spur nicknamed Small Beer and trying at least to make them nervous on the higher peak called Brandy. "Without artillery or mortars," an English officer reflects, also with professional detachment, "I'd need two battalions to take the high one. The only way the Greeks will get there is to bring in some heavy stuff or go up at night with knives and take their casualties."

By a combination of telephone calls back to the area commander at the next village and old-fashioned shouts up and down the mountainside, I get permission from the Turks to climb up the face of Brandy and talk to the two men manning an old British Second World War pillbox there.

The soldier on duty willingly enough shows me his rifle, stencilled Property of the U.S. Government, and says he has no more idea where it came from than I have. No, he hasn't fired it today. Unlike the cowardly Greeks, who stick their heads down, hold their weapons high and let their rifle bullets fly with the looping trajectory of a mortar, he disdains to fire blind. As for the politics of the situation there is for him one solution and only one – final and absolute partition. "I am a member of the army of Cyprus," he says. "I soldiered beside Greek Cypriots for three years. I will never soldier beside them again. I will never live beside them. Do you know why? Because I hate them. That is why! I hate them. I will always hate them. I will hate them until I die."

Later a drive through two more roadblocks – one of each – to talk to the Greek soldiers at the base of Gin mountain. No, they haven't been shooting today. But a lot of wild fire from the Turks has been coming in on them. The Turks, they explain bitterly, are afraid of a real battle; they get their heads low and their muzzles high, and let fly at anything that moves; Greek, UN or – this with more relish than seems called for – visiting journalists.

Historical Note: For its size (about thirty-five hundred square miles) and its population (about six hundred thousand) Cyprus has a fantastic overburden of scar tissue. It lies in a cul-de-sac of the eastern Mediterranean where Africa meets Asia Minor and Asia Minor meets Europe. It has never been quite small enough for the passers-by to ignore or large enough for them to avoid through respect or fear. The pre-Christian conquerors and partial conquerors included the Egyptians, the Assyrians, the Greeks, the Hittites, the Phœnicians, the Persians, the Macedonians and the Romans. Later occupants and partial occupants have included the Crusaders, the Genoese, the Venetians, the Franks, the Turks and the British. There has never been a time in the last four thousand years when Cyprus hasn't been at war or on the verge of war or recovering from a war. It's had trade wars, holy wars, political wars, wars of brutal accident, wars of naked pillage, wars of chivalry, wars of dark

144

revenge, wars of liberation, wars of enslavement. It's always had a war of some kind, or else a war's prospect or a war's fresh memory.

SUNDAY

It starts to rain heavily around noon and the weekend Nimrods pack up and start home early to get over their ouzo and Keo-brandy hangovers, like dejected picnickers. By nightfall it's dead quiet all over the island.

Historical Note: It is not necessary to believe in Aphrodite or Adonis to believe in Cyprus as a dwelling place and a fortress for the gods and God. The gospels say that St. Paul landed here in A.D. 45 and it was here that St. Barnabas, his companion, founded the oldest of the Orthodox Christian churches. There is a final tomb of Lazarus in the seaside town of Larnaca. One of the few really successful Jewish Pogroms against the Christians – two hundred thousand killed – took place in Cyprus in the second century. Thanks to capricious winds and King Richard's determination to rescue his shipwrecked Berengaria, the island became the sally-port for the Crusades. None of its shrines is more sacred than the resting place of the Lady Umm Haram, and no story more touching than the story of her death. She had come to Cyprus with the Mohammed's own blessing on an Arab crusade some four hundred years before the time of Richard. Then, the translated inscription reads, "The holy woman (may God be pleased with her!) was set with all honour on a mule; and on arriving at the place where her luminous tomb is seen, they were attacked by Genoese infidels, and falling from her beast she broke her pellucid neck and yielded up her victorious soul, and in that fragrant spot at once was buried."

MONDAY

The shooting war slackens off but the much more deadly and complex war of politics – the ceaseless grinding of wheels within wheels and other wheels within the wheels within – starts to gather pace. Archbishop Makarios, the President of the island and the spiritual leader and generalissimo of four fifths of its inhabitants, is in Athens. His aims are the whole world's secret: 1. to see whether the Greek government wants him to step up the military campaign, 2. to see whether the Greek government wants him to throw his whole weight once more behind the old Greek-Cypriot dream of Enosis – union with Greece, 3. to sound out the prospect of bringing back the legendary old guerrilla king, George Grivas, and putting him in charge of liquidating the Turkish military once and for all and swiftly.

The most popular guesses on the island are:

1. The Greek-Greeks will instruct Makarios and the Cyprus-Greeks to go on playing it relatively cool. If they make it much rougher on the Cyprus-Turks it's entirely possible that the Turk-Turks will invade, as they were threatening to do when the trouble broke out last December. Although there is a strong tendency in Nicosia as well as Athens and Ankara to think of Greek-Turk wars in terms of 1821, 1897 and 1922 (Turkey won two of those and Greece won one), there is also a growing awareness that the North Atlantic Treaty Organization could be the next major casualty.

2. For somewhat the same reasons, Greece will urge Makarios to forget Enosis for now and, some predict, forever.

3. Makarios will make it seem that he wants Grivas to come back to Cyprus. He will also offer conditions that Grivas can't or won't accept. In the bloodstained, cloak-and-dagger years of E.O.K.A. and the war of "liberation" against the British, the island was big enough to hold them both (or to be strictly accurate to hold their shadows; Grivas was a refugee with a huge price on his head and Makarios was an exile). But now, in 1964, there's only room at the top for one. The schoolboys are parading in Metaxas Square for the return of Grivas and minor politicians and leaders are signing petitions. But the smart money says that when Black Mak comes back from Greece he'll come back alone and he'll come back still as boss.

I spend most of this day of guesswork and speculation in the company of a Turk who is determined to show me the evidence of the atrocities of last December, down to the carefully preserved bloodstains in the famous bathtub, the bits of hair and human brain still clinging to the walls. "I hope Grivas does come," he says. And there is no doubting that he means it. "He will start another massacre of our people and then at last Turkey will stop looking on."

Historical Note: During the E.O.K.A. *troubles – the reign of terror in which Makarios was the dark and silken eminence and Grivas the enforcer – the known list of killed, from 1955 through 1958 was 218 Greeks, 142 British and 27 Turks. For a Greek to help the British maintain what was left of the law was equivalent to his death sentence. The Turks became the strongest civil ally of the British. The prudent Turkish auxiliaries, some of them have told me in the last few days, began laying away British guns and ammunition against the rainy day that has always come before and always comes again. By the time the British abdicated in 1960 both the Turk and Greek communities had four extra years in which to reinforce their arsenals. The next three years – the first years of a struggle for common sense and tolerance under an almost criminally insane constitution – did nothing to arrest the process. When Makarios announced the end of the Turks' minority rights last November and the fighting started in December, everybody proceeded to his battle station like an actor in a tableau* déjà vu. *It might have been the Arabs versus the Genoese, the Saracens versus the Knights Hospitaller, the gallant Helenes of Byron's time against the cruel, despotic Sultan or the vengeful garrisons of the Dardanellese poised to march on Smyrna. But this time there was no nonesense about chivalry.*

TUESDAY

Makarios comes back from Greece, as predicted, alone. Much kissing of the archiepiscopal ring under the camera floodlights at the airport. Much bestowing of the archiepiscopal smile. *Historical Note: Every now and then an exasperated student of* real-politik *suggests the only practical solution is to fence the island off, to tow it out through the straits of Gibraltar and sink it, or sell it to the highest bidder, or give it away to anyone who is willing to take it. This last has been tried many times, but it has never worked. It is a simple, sober statement of fact that Cyprus has been given away more times than any other colony or dominion since the beginning of time. Marc Antony once gave the island to Cleopatra as a love trinket. Having conquered it more or less against his will back in the twelfth century old Coeur de Lion soon found it a white*

147

elephant and gave it to the crusading brotherhood, the Knights Templar. The Templars very quickly gave it back. Then the widowed and dispossessed consort of a queen of Jerusalem came by and Richard gave the island to him. For the next seven hundred years it changed hands only by acts of war. But in 1878 it was given away again – this time by Turkey to Britain. Theoretically the Turks remained the sovereign power but Britain acquired all the military, administrative and taxing rights in return for a guarantee that they would protect the Turks against the Russians and a further guarantee that the goat-herds of Cyprus would continue paying their annual tribute to Istanbul.

In 1914 when Britain and Turkey found themselves at war against each other Britain wiped out the arrangement and annexed the island wholly. A year later, when the campaign was going badly in the Balkans, Britain offered to give Cyprus to Greece if Greece would enter the war on Britain's side. The Greeks refused. When at last, and for the first time in its four thousand years of recorded history, Cyprus was finally given to the Cypriots in 1960 there were so many strings attached that the island ended up with not one master but three. Britain kept two military bases to protect itself at Suez and elsewhere in the Mediterranean. Turkey and Greece both were given the right to keep military contingents on the island. The thing the Cyprus-Greeks have yearned for throughout the last two centuries – Enosis, union with Greece – was specifically forbidden by the constitution. The thing the Turks cherish as their last line of defence – Taksim, partition – was specifically forbidden too. But the real time bombs in the constitution were the clauses that gave the Turkish twenty per cent the right to veto the administrative and legislative proposals of the Greek eighty per cent. The rules under which Cyprus became an "independent" republic within the commonwealth might have been written by Alice's friend, the Dodo: "Everybody has won and all must have prizes."

WEDNESDAY

Just after breakfast a fusillade of small-arms fire pours into and around the leafy gardens of the Ledra Palace hotel. This inflicts no casualties, but quickly disperses the Greek workmen who have been trying to build a swimming pool and who have obviously been mistaken by the nearby Turks for a crew of soldiers building another pillbox. During the lull I go up to the second floor, planning to get my binoculars. My room turns out to be locked from the inside. Just along the hallway a stiff-lipped young English subaltern of the UN Peace Force is ordering a reluctant gunner to get out on the roof and observe.

"Observe, sir?" the gunner says.

"Yes, Jones, get out there on the roof and observe. On the double now."

"Yes, sir. Is there anything I should observe in particular, sir?"

"Come on now, Jones, don't ask silly questions. Get out there on the roof."

"Yes, sir. Any particular part of the roof, sir?"

"Just get out there on the roof, Jones. On the double, now."

"Yes, sir. Someone seems to be shooting, sir."

"Of course someone seems to be shooting. Get out there and they will stop. On the double, now."

Gunner Jones finally proceeds, unenthusiastically, in the general direction of the roof, and I obtain entry to my room. A Greek guerrilla in a blue turtle-neck sweater is kneeling behind the bed. He has a Lee-Enfield rifle and three boxes of ammunition and is preparing to start shooting out the northern window at the Turkish machine-gun post slightly more than a hundred yards up the road .The floor porter, the chambermaid and the floor waiter are grouped behind him, opening the ammunition and shouting encouragement to him, and getting in and out of my way in some fantastic, Chaplinesque hope that if they distract my attention sufficiently I may not notice what is going on. Through the door-way I hear the British subaltern giving a final, strangled ultimatum to Gunner Jones. "Come on now, Jones, on the double."

"Very good, sir."

I hear my own voice, calm, precise, controlled. "Now look here! Really! Now see here! After all. . . !"

The Greek hotel porter raises a clenched fist. "We must have the revenge!" he cries. "The revenge!"

The man with the gun solves everything, at least temporarily, by gathering up his little munitions pile and fleeing for the base-ment. In the hallway he and the officer of Gunner Jones exchange a look of utter bafflement. Along the corridor in the other corner room, the military secretary of the UN commander-in-chief returns from his breakfast to find his room half full of sandbags. The Battle of the Ledra Palace had begun.

Historical Note: Besides being the meeting-place of three continents, a dozen religions and at least as many cultures, Cyprus is an heir of two of the great schools of human torture – middle-age European and Oriental. When the Venetian, Marcantonio Bragadino, surrendered Famagusta in 1571, the conquering Turks, who had promised him his freedom, cut off his ears and nose, hung him outside the city gates for two weeks and finally skinned him, still alive. During the massacres of 1821 a spiritual ancestor of Archbishop Makarios was saddled like a horse and ridden around the streets of Nicosia until his Turkish oppressors got tired and cut his head off. The Crusaders, the Egyptians, the Franks and the Greeks weren't always so inventive but at heart they were no more squeamish.

THURSDAY

Two Greeks shot dead on Ledra Street. For a while the centre of activity has moved away from the hotel and the mountains to the famous Murder Mile of the 1950's.

Historical Note: Many of the great mosques of Cyprus are former Christian churches. These were seized not from the Orthodox Church but from the Church of Rome – which went under with the collapse of the Crusades and, also, of the Franks and the Venetians. Religion, relatively speaking – and if any of their differences can be said to be minor – is a fairly minor point of friction between the Turk and Greek Cypriots. An earnest Turkish businessman tried to explain it to me. "I loathe and detest the Greeks and they loathe and detest me. But it's not because they are Christians and I am a Muslim. It's because they are Greeks and I am a Turk. As far as religion is concerned they could be Methodists or Buddhists and it wouldn't make the slightest difference to me. But they are Greeks. They burned down my house last December. Twenty of them, in full view of the boy who was to marry her, raped a girl I know. They are Greeks and I am a Turk and I wish that every one of them was dead."

FRIDAY

Another quiet day. Keeping track here is getting more and more like the night police-beat back in Winnipeg. Check the blotter, check the first aid stations, check the hospitals and call the desk and say nothing doing. At the third Turkish barricade the slender boy who usually waves me through lifts his gun. "Those Greeks," he says, "are shooting at the road again. Have you been to Omorphita?"

"Yes, I was there the other day."

"Have you been to the village of Hammit Keuy?"

"Yes, I have been there too."

"Are the people there well?"

"There is no sickness and no hunger, they are crowded but there is no hunger or sickness."

"I have a sister and a mother there. Is there any happiness there?"

"Perhaps a little." I am now aware that I have begun to sound more pointless and irrelevant by the minute, like Colonel Blimp or a missionary to Samoa. It's a relief to us both when he tells me to go on down the road.

Historical Note: Alexander the Great was one of the early conquerors, Shakespeare's "seaport in Cyprus" was Famagusta and Othello's Tower is still there. Local color is in abundant supply everywhere and sometimes unexpectedly. One late afternoon I deliberately lost myself in the narrow maze of Nicosia's Turkish city. I turned another corner and there in an open doorway was a woman as round and benign as Man Mountain Dean, smiling owlishily behind half an acre of mascara, henna and silken veils, and holding out her jeweled hands. Three corners later I found a UN sentry who directed me back to the occidental safety of the Ledra Palace.

SATURDAY

The Turks have been dejected. Not beaten, for to be beaten now means, as they see it, the same as being dead. But overnight they take new heart. Ankara radio has announced that from now on the Green Line must be considered the southern frontier of Turkey, in short that Turkey will fight for Cyprus. Coincidentally some additional weapons – not very good ones but additional ones – have started showing up on the Turkish side. The daily Turkish "news release" devotes a third of its front page to the black poster cry: Taksim.

Historical Note: There are four mountains called Olympus between Athens and Istanbul and two of them are on Cyprus.

A visit with the famous E.O.K.A. killer, Nicos Sampson. Starting as a newspaper copy boy back in the 1950's and riding his bike to work Sampson shot somewhere between ten and twenty-five British soldiers in the back before they caught him and sentenced him to death. He was pardoned and then granted amnesty and now, still in his twenties, he owns the island's largest and slickest newspaper, its largest stable of racehorses and some of its most violent memories. We meet in the directors' room of the Nicosia Race Club, in the genteel surroundings in which a visiting journalist might meet an E.P. Taylor at Woodbine or a royal duke at Ascot. Sampson rolls up his trouser legs to show the scars of torture and grabs my hand and runs it down the corrugations of his head. He holds out his fingers to show where the nails have been slashed back and burned. I ask this toughest and most durable and merciless of all the old E.O.K.A. killers where and when he thinks the present war will end. "War?" he says. "We have no war here. We have a mutiny in the army. A rebellion in the civil service. We have treason among the Turks. But we do not have a war."

I try to get Sampson talking about the earlier realities of his strange and desperate life but in his new respectability it is largely a waste of time. All he wants to discuss is George Washington, Mahatma Gandhi, the healthy state of the national economy, and his horse's chances in the third.

Historical Note: This is a cynical and an ugly thought and it does scant justice to the people who have died, will die or will drag out their days in an Eden turned to desert. Nevertheless it's true, and there's no escaping it, that the island's most salable export is trouble and its best cash crop is cash. Although on the green mountain slopes the land looks fair and fertile it does not even sustain itself in food. Its copper mines are almost exhausted, its fisheries have never produced. Catering to the occupying garrisons has been for decades and still is the industry that keeps Cyprus from bankruptcy. The biggest single manufacturing employer in Cyprus is the Coca-Cola company. The biggest chain of stores is N.A.A.F.I. – the traditional grog shop and tuck shop of the British serviceman. If by any wild chance Cyprus ever found itself without native or visiting warriors its natural deficit economy would become an economy of utter disaster.

As it is the national bank declared a monumental dividend of sixteen per cent in 1963; the import-export figures, thanks partly to the growing popularity of the excellent Cyprus wines, were better in the first three months of 1964 than they had been in years and the island has just launched a series of new social-welfare schemes. Next only to Israel's, everyone concedes that the standard of living in Cyprus is the highest in the Mediterranean.

MONDAY

Major Pat Tremblay of the Van Doos lets me come along on a helicopter mission to Brandy mountain. It is very quiet, very still. A few vultures hang above the mountain top and above them an eagle looks around. Tremblay lands and sits down on a thorn rock. In a short while the thorn bushes and scrub olives start to part and a few Turk soldiers come out, bearded and unkempt, tired, bleary, dirty and tough, but not in the least uncertain. They sit down around us, with their old Sten guns and M-1's and Lee-Enfields across their knees.

The commander, a gaunt young man in a baseball cap, speaks some English but prefers to use his deputy as an interpreter. Tremblay sits for a while. Then he says, casually, "There's been quite a lot of shooting down there at the chicken farm."

The deputy translates. "Yes," the commander says.

"I wish there was some way to stop it," Tremblay says.

"Yes."

"I'm down there, you know. I've got some of my men down there all the time. I've got an armoured car down there and every time anybody shoots down there they're shooting at me. And then of course there are a lot of women trying to go to work on the farm and everytime there's any shooting in that direction, well, they get scared."

"Yes."

"Well then, how would it be if you just stopped shooting down there at the chicken farm? You're shooting at me and you're shooting at these Greek women and it would be better for everybody if you stopped. I know you don't want to hit me and I know you don't want to hit the Greek women but you're shooting at us and it would be better if you stopped."

The commander confers with his deputy. "We have never fired one shot at the chicken farm. If anything came near you it must have been fired by the Greeks."

153

"Well," Tremblay says, "suppose you just stopped firing anything in that direction at all. Then if anything came in near me or near the women we'd all know it was the Greeks."

"Yes," the commander says. "But what about the boulder down there?"

"Well, I'm going down to see about that as soon as we're finished here."

The Turk grows more communicative. "They keep shooting at us and then sometimes they try to climb up the mountain under the cover of the boulder. That is why we shoot. We never shoot at you. We never shoot at the women. If you can get them to stop shooting from the boulder or stop them coming up from behind it we'll stop shooting too."

We transfer from the helicopter to a jeep and, though the elapsed air and ground mileage is twenty times that much, arrive a mile away among the Greeks behind the boulder. Same beards, same worn but not too bad sub-machine guns, same sandbags and barbed wire. Same undertaking: "If they will stop we will stop."

"They have promised to stop," Tremblay says.

"They are without honour. Their promises are useless."

"Let's try it anyway," Tremblay suggests.

"All right we'll try it." For several hours there is no shooting on either side. But in late afternoon it starts again; who began or why no one will ever have the slightest idea.

Historical Note: During much of the three hundred years of Turkish rule, the two main communities lived not precisely in a state of friendship but in a non-enmity born of their common misery. The Muslim sultans, grand viziers and pashas decided it would not be good tactics to suppress the autocephalous Christian church. Instead they made the church their agent and administrator. Throughout most of the sixteenth, seventeenth and eighteenth centuries the bishops and archbishops collected the taxes, kept as much as they could for themselves and the Holy Mother and passed the balance on to Constantinople. For a long time Cyprus was sold to the highest bidder from year to year, like a hat-check concession. A British consular official, Alexander Drummond, once made an inventory of the Establishment. The officials he identified included the Musselim, or chief administrator and tax collector; the Mufti, or supreme judge; the Molla, or deputy judge and deputy administrator;

*the Nagibu'l Eshraf, the senior decendant of Mahomet; the
Divan Effendi, or high chancellor; the Khaznadar or high
treasurer; the Ich-agaler, the grooms of the bedchamber and
pages of honour; the Embrakhor, or master of the horse;
the Oahveji, the coffee-maker; the Bukhardanji, the per-
fumer and keeper of the aloes; the Bash Chawush, the keeper
of prisoners; the Alay Chawush, the court buffoon; and many
others.*

TUESDAY

A pleasant talk with the man who has been given the task of
mediating the basic issues and arriving at a solution acceptable to
everybody here in Cyprus as well as to everybody in the much
more complicated battleground on the East River in New York.
Sakari Tuomaija is a big, Wagner-opera Finn, a man of immense
good will and hard experience who has somehow helped his own
little country to survive in the face of odds almost as hopeless as
the odds now facing Cyprus. It is betraying no secrets to say that
up to now the mediator has discovered no ray of light. We have
agreed I won't quote him on anything that is "substantive," but as
I'm leaving he asks if I'd like to take down one thing. It doesn't
make very newsy or original copy but here it is: "If there is any
way at all for mankind to settle the much more difficult and
complicated problems that are open to it elsewhere, then this
relatively simple problem of Cyprus can be and will be settled."

*Historical Note: One of the few concerted and united actions
of the Greek Cypriots and the Turkish Cypriots occurred in
1743. Alexander Drummond, the British consul, summar-
ized the incident and its background. "The archbishop, with
the countenance of the Musselim who shared in the robbery,
levied from the poor people no less than forty thousand
piastres; but they complained so effectively to the Porte (the
Turkish government) corroborating their complaints with
bribery, that he was stripped of archiepiscopal robes, dignity
and emoluments. Indeed, there is no difficulty in obtaining
this kind of satisfaction, for nothing is more agreeable to
those corrupt ministers than complaints, because both
plaintiffs and defendants enforce their arguments with pres-
ents, which must be renewed every hearing. And if the
plaintiff gains his point so far as to make an empty saddle,*

155

the whole profit accrues to these ministers, who not only sell the vacant place to the best bidder, but afterwards share in the plunder of the new purchaser."

WEDNESDAY

Archbishop Makarios will see me at the presidential palace at 5:30. I go a little early, not sure how long I'll be held up by the guards, and have a good twenty minutes to stroll among the flower gardens, the empty tennis-courts and the disused swimming pool. The lion and the unicorn still stand guard above the entrance, as they did, unsuccessfully, for the departed British governors.

This is the first time I have seen Makarios without his tall archbishop's hat and it's a surprise to discover that even though the famous electric beard is as impressive close up as at a distance, the archbishop is growing bald. Today he wears a blue silk robe. The only jewelry, besides the archiepiscopal ring, is a small diamond collar-piece. He sits behind a large executive's desk in an office almost identical with the office of, say, the mayor of Edmonton or the chairman of the board of a Bay Street brokerage firm. There are no ikons and there is no incense and the only Byzantine note is lent by a grey and mauve cat that wanders back and forth between the feet of the archbishop and the feet of his interpreter.

Makarios uses the interpreter only when he is reaching for some shade of meaning. He speaks carefully, slowly and softly. He smiles all the time – a forced and mirthless, automatic smile. I can't help wondering where I've seen it before. And then it comes. This is very much the smile of another of the world's great negotiators and manipulators – Premier W.A.C. Bennett of British Columbia.

Makarios talks freely and without reservations. The only time he seems in the least uneasy is when I ask about Grivas. "That is a bad question," he says, and the smile disappears. But it returns. "There are so many causes of strife here. The Greek government pointed out to me and I agreed that for Grivas to come back now would add more strife. For the time being he will not return."

As for Enosis, that too can wait. "We must always consider," he says, "whether Greece wants Enosis. That is by no means sure. Then we can decide whether Cyprus wants Enosis. First we must have self-government and self-determination and above all we must have peace."

156

Historical Note: A hundred and fifty years ago a Catalan traveler tried to sum up the position of the religious hierarchy. "The Greeks are extremely submissive towards their bishops; in saluting them they bow low, take off their caps and hold them before them upside down. . . . For this community of slaves the bishops are rallying points. It is through them that it preserves some kind of existence, so that it suits the people to give to their prelates political importance, such as even the Turks allow to them."

THURSDAY

An interview with Markarios' arch-enemy, the Turkish leader, Dr. Fazil Kutchuk. In contrast to Makarios' poised and silken elegance, Kutchuk wears a crumpled, tieless, slightly soiled white Arrow shirt beneath his slept-in jacket. He is unshaven and his hand shakes a little between his cigarette and his cup of Turkish coffee.

It is one of the conditions of our interview that I submit some questions first and allow Dr. Kutchuk to answer them in writing. The last one – are the Cypriots really willing to risk atomic war? – produces answer 5: "It is not for me to answer what the Turkish contingent in Cyprus will do if the Greeks attack it. This is an answer for the Turkish government to give. As far as I know the Turkish government has already declared that she will regard an attack on the Turkish contingent on Cyprus as an attack on Turkey itself. It is, therefore, for the Greeks to consider this matter twice before they take such an action as would jeopardize the world peace."

Kutchuk leans forward. "You have talked to Makarios?"

"Yes."

"You were impressed by him?"

"I have heard," I say, "that you consider him no more than a murderer. Is that true?"

Kutchuk looks over to his interpreter and then waits so there will be no chance of misquotation. "I have no doubt in my mind that the main perpetrator and the man behind the E.O.K.A. and the present troubles was Makarios. You may find out for yourself whether he is a murderer or not. To me it is very obvious, very clear."

"Then do you see no chance of making an arrangement with Makarios and the Greeks?"

"Yes. We will have partition."

157

"And if they won't accept it?"

"Then to the last man. To the last – " Kutchuk looks at his interpreter.

"To the last breath."

"Yes. To the last breath."

Historical Note: The moon is a perfect crescent but Venus is far away. The voice of the muezzin echoes from the twin minarets of San Sophia, but the muezzin no longer has to make the climb in person: General Electric.

Tanri Uludur
Tanri Uludur
Tanri Dan Baska . . .
Yoktur Tapacat
Haydayin Namaza
Haydayin Felaha
God is good.
God is good.
God is munificent.
There is no other God to pray to.

From 1960 to 1964, Ralph Allen spent six months of each year as a contributing editor on *Maclean's* and the other six working on his own books. He had already published, besides *Homemade Banners* (Longmans, Green, 1946), *The Chartered Libertine,* (Macmillan, 1954), a satire on Canadian broadcasting, and *Peace River Country* (Doubleday, 1958), a gentle novel about a prairie family that was his own favourite among his books and the Literary Guild selection for the month of its publication. (He once told a student who was using the book as the basis of a graduate thesis that he wrote it "as an expression of my belief that what striving people do to reach a better life or an end in life is sometimes as fruitful as the end itself – even when they may never in fact reach that end.")

After he left the *Maclean's* editorial chair he set to work on *Ordeal By Fire* (Doubleday, 1961), a history of Canada during the period from 1910 to 1945, a mammoth work of research which he turned into a lively chronicle of a time that he knew well. Next he wrote, in quick succession, *Ask The Name Of The Lion* (Doubleday, 1962), a short novel based on his experiences reporting the war in the Congo, and a long novel *The High White Forest* (Doubleday, 1964) which drew on his Winnipeg newspaper days and World War II experiences.

After this last book was dispatched to his publishers in New York in the spring of 1964, he had to make a difficult decision about his future. His arrangement with *Maclean's* was coming up for review, his publishers had asked him to sign a contract for three more books, the Southam newspaper chain wanted him to become their roving foreign correspondent, and the *Toronto Daily Star* was offering him the managing editorship of that paper.

One morning in June, he telephoned Gillis Purcell, general manager of the Canadian Press and his closest friend, and told him he wanted to see him at noon to talk over a problem. When they met, Allen began characteristically by saying, "Look, I don't want any goddam advice, I just want to talk." By the time they had finished talking an hour or so later, although Allen would not say if or what he had decided, Purcell knew him well enough to realize he was going to make the hardest choice and become the *Star*'s managing editor.

What he was taking on was the equivalent, in the newspaper business, of ten rounds with Jack Dempsey in his prime. The *Toronto Daily Star,* the biggest newspaper in Canada, had a flamboyant history, and was considered in the trade to be the toughest place in the country for a newspaperman to work. (An old hand once said with some feeling, "the fields of Canadian journalism are white with the bones of men who have tried to make it on the *Star.*")

It had long come under the influence of two hard, opinionated and disparate men, Joseph Atkinson, the founder, and Harry Hindmarsh, his son-in-law and throughout its history, had been the scene of much infighting and conflict.

In 1964, the editor and assistant publisher was Beland Honderich, the paper's onetime financial columnist, a man of serious purpose and liberal opinion, who was restlessly seeking a managing editor to help him realize his dream of making the *Star* into a great and respected paper that would have an important influence not just in metropolitan Toronto but on the national scene. In Ralph Allen, he found that man.

During the two years Allen was on the *Star,* he had an impact that was far out of proportion to the time he spent there. Under his leadership, the paper expanded its coverage of both national and international affairs, and adopted a style of reporting that put more emphasis on probing analysis than flashy newsbreaks. (Although there was probably nothing flashier in the history of Canadian journalism than the *Star*'s discovery of Hal Banks and Gerda Munsinger, scoops that both appeared under the byline of a great reporter, Robert Reguly, but were master-minded every step of the way by Ralph Allen.)

He also had an influence on the morale of the *Star*'s staff that was to outlast his brief tenure. "Other bright men have come to the *Star,* men whose ambitions were for themselves," said Gregory Clark, a onetime *Star* employee and a wise man who had spent a long lifetime observing the Canadian newspaper scene. "But Ralph went there, as he went everywhere else, not with ambitions

160

for himself but with ambitions for what he was working on. He was tough and yet somehow innocent; and a curious, indefinable quality radiated from him, a down-right, down-to-earth honesty that couldn't help but affect the people who worked under him."

Most of Ralph's creative effort in the period just before he died was expended on the *Star*'s news pages, on the personal memos he wrote to individual employees and the general memos he posted almost daily on the editorial-room bulletin board. But he did manage to get away from the paper in the fall of 1965 to spend nearly six weeks covering the Viet Nam war and he also contributed several reminiscences and opinion pieces, some of which are included here. When these pieces were published in the *Star,* there appeared under his byline only *"Star Staff writer,"* a slug that was used for all reporters on his staff; he once explained this by saying, "I would hate people to think the only reason I could get anything published was that I'm passing judgment on myself."

CANADA NEEDS AN OBEROMBUDSMAN

(May 15, 1965)

Every time you pick up a newspaper or a magazine or turn on a radio or television set these days you run into some crusader saying that what this country needs is an ombudsman.

The ombudsman is a magic supernumerary, a person outside the normal apparatus and control of government. His role is to protect the innocent from the state.

That's great. The innocent need protecting. In addition to the ombudsman shielding and cherishing the innocent, do we not need a kind of "oberombudsman" to watch and if need be prosecute the guilty?

A lot of us are starting to wonder about the guilty. How long are they going to continue getting away with it?

Everyone who can read knows that our laws have failed to protect us against malefactors and incompetents in our highest professions and institutions.

Under the disguise of "self-policing" we have allowed some doctors to get away, quite literally, with murder. We have allowed law societies to sustain and tolerate men in very high office who would not ordinarily be allowed in any decent man's back yard. We have permitted men to continue in the cabinet ranks of politics whom any self-respecting truck driver would not talk to on the street. The stock markets and the brokerage business harbour, to use a euphemism, far too many thieves.

My oberombudsman would try to correct some of this.

He would not wait for George McClellan, Commissioner of the R.C.M.P., to work out his further reflection and testimony on why he hasn't found Lucien Rivard. He would get rough on this question, because that would be his job as oberombudsman. Whatever explanation George McClellan gave him, the oberombudsman would explain right back that he wasn't looking for explanations. He was looking for Rivard. He would get Rivard.

George LeMay, under the oberombudsman, would scarcely have been able to live in a yacht in Fort Lauderdale for several months while he was wanted in Canada on a criminal charge.

Hal Banks would not have been able to live on another yacht while escaping Canadian justice. It would not have been necessary for the *Toronto Daily Star* to go and find him while the Canadian Department of Justice had lost him and has now conveniently lost him again. It would not be necessary to continue reminding the officials of the Canadian Department of Justice that one of their functions is to bring criminals to justice, or try at least.

If there were an oberombudsman some fairly pertinent questions would have been asked about why a notorious hood like Rivard walked out of a Canadian prison as if he were a passing tourist.

An oberombudsman would want to know who is looking into the affairs of the Law Society of Upper Canada and see who is policing them and how and whether the officers are really working in the public interest or their own.

He would look into the affairs of the Canadian Medical Association and try to satisfy himself that these are in order and that the public interest is being protected.

He would look, particularly into the stock exchange.

What he would be told is that everything is in the hands of the authorities. A proper oberombudsman would not believe this. The oberombudsman would hound the guilty, the lazy, the venial – whether they were doctors, brokers, lawyers, bankers, or news-papermen – as relentlessly as the ombudsman is supposed to guard the innocent. He would nail about eighty per cent of the people who now escape or hide behind influential friends.

My oberombudsman would be as nasty as Inspector Javert pursuing Jean Valjean. Nasty or not, he'd clean things up a great deal. We need him.

WHY I WON'T ARGUE BICULTURALISM WITH ANYBODY ANY MORE

(May 19, 1965)

Open letter to Mr. G.R.S. Hawkins,
Executive Director,
Canadian Institute on Public Affairs
Dear Mr. Hawkins,

Thanks for your invitation to debate the question of English-French relations at the forthcoming Couchiching conference.

I am most flattered to know that two of the other people you had thought of inviting were Claude Ryan of *Le Devoir* and Gerard Pelletier, recently of *La Presse*. I do not know of two more distinguished journalists in our country.

The trouble, from my point of view, is that either of these gentlemen would slay me in an open debate. I would lose my temper or, worse, go to sleep. I find the continued dispute about the French and English in Canada so exasperating that it drives me either to fury or total boredom.

I know that Messrs. Ryan and Pelletier cannot be associated with the left-over mercenaries of the *ancien régime,* who have been exacerbating our old blood feud. I am sure that if we could get locked up privately in a hotel room or a fishing boat they might agree with my contention that nowhere in the world has any defeated minority been better treated than have the French-Canadians in Canada. I would likely agree with them that nowhere has a fat, secure majority been less sensitive towards the feelings though not the rights and welfare of its victims.

But any public discussion with them would still be a waste of time. I would be expected to beat my breast and cry *mea culpa!* and frankly I'm fed up with that. They would consider it their duty to charge me with sins that neither I nor my ancestors ever committed against them or their ancestors and I would consider it my duty to plead guilty to them and offer to put them right.

We would end up in the coils of the B and B commission and if I may say, sir, I say the Hell with it.

I have strong feelings about Canada, by the way. Not, however, so strong that I intend to let them become a source of endlesss humiliation. I am not among those who believe that Canada was created by God. It became a nation because of the vainglory of the English; because of the treachery of the French (who could have protected their colonists easily); because of the incompetence of the Americans (who were on the verge of capturing the country twice); and because of the enslavement and virtual extinction of the Hurons, Iroquois and Algonquins.

No matter what we choose to say of it, Canada is a whole series of accidents. If it should expire in its present form the world would survive and so, almost certainly, would Canada's separate parts. I don't expect my children to suffer much if Quebec should withdraw from Canada or Canada withdraw from Quebec.

Yet it's been a lovely place to grow up in, whether it was an accident or not. I don't pretend to know every foot of it, but every foot of it I know has a meaning. The places I know go from Labrador to Hudson Bay, through the great silent wastes of the prairies where I grew up and on through the tundra to the Northwest Territories and then across the mountains to the great turquoise wash of the Pacific.

It has been a good place while we have had the sense to cling to it. But I will not debate its future. If it goes, God bless it! No talking I can do will change a thing. The one real chance of saving Canada lies in its heart and its loins.

But I do appreciate your invitation and regret that I must decline it.

Yours sincerely,

RALPH ALLEN

(September 23, 1965)

SAIGON – *Sex and the Saigon Girl* is a best-seller that never will be written. And that may well represent one of the most poignant of all the failures of communications between East and West.

Millions of words have been printed about the combined love affair, sparring match and confidence game in constant progress between the five thousand or so bar girls and the two hundred thousand or so male foreign devils who have passed this way during the last three or four years.

They've all been written by, in behalf of, as a warning to, or a kind of field manual for the parties of the second part. Nobody, to the best of my knowledge, has ever made a serious attempt to appraise the matter from the minority or distaff point of view.

It's not that there's any need to question the basic facts. There probably are five thousand bar girls in Saigon and there may even be as many as ten thousand.

Almost all of them are passable and some are beautiful.

They manage somehow to convey the demure and giggly innocence of a troop of Brownies on their first midnight taffy-pull with the iron persistence of Charlotte Whitton on a television panel.

It's true that by playing on the clean-cut American lusts of the clean-cut American GI they have converted enough U.S. dollars into cold tea to equip another medium-sized battle fleet and a squadron of strategic bombers. It may be that they have done even worse, but prudence draws a veil.

The one incontestable fact is that the Saigon girl's angle on this has been largely overlooked.

It has to be assumed that any of the confidences she bestows on the foreign devil are as little to be trusted as her method of dealing gin rummy – a diversion she pretends to have been addicted to since her early girlhood. Gin rummy is the Saigon girl's equivalent of the old-fashioned Klondyke girl's three-card monte. The least it can do is keep the client at the bar and buying.

The real block to a satisfactory dialogue between the hostesses and the patrons of the numerous *bistros* here may, however, boil down to nothing more insidious than the difference of language.

All the girls get their English out of a guide-book especially written for bar girls and all the GI's get their Vietnamese out of a guidebook written for GI's.

The bar girls' handbook is considerably more realistic than the GI's handbook, which is founded on the ancient Thomas Cook and Sons, Berlitz and American Express superstition that when any American gets into a strange country all he wants to do is buy a pair of shoes or start haggling over the price of a taxi.

The only English-Vietnamese manual I have been able to find on the open market is a volume called *Easy Vietnamese for You.* It is written by the local scholar, Tran-Buu-Duc, and enthusiastically endorsed by several American officials here, one of whom says it is "a frequent reference of AID teams working in the field, as well as a constant help to the U.S. foreign service officer."

A GI with whom I am friendly told me that he too had trouble establishing any kind of an intellectual rapport with the indigenous female so I loaned him my copy of *Easy Vietnamese for You.*

After a day or so's preliminary study he repaired to one of the little bars on Tu-Do Street. The following conversation took place, with the GI referring surreptitiously to his Vietnamese manual from one side of the bar and his vis-à-vis sneaking quick glances at her English book from the other.

SHE: Hello. How are You?

HE: Toi mon di den toa. Sat sir My, sau do ri ren nha Buru dien. (I want to go to the American Embassy and after that, to the Post Office.)

SHE: You buy me a drink?

HE: Goi nay dan tem bao nhieu? (What is the postage for this parcel?)

SHE: I'm very lonely. Are you lonely?

HE: Dien tin gap bao nhieu mot chur? (What is the charge for an urgent telegram?)

SHE: Nobody loves me.

HE: Toi nuon mua it tem. (I want to have some postage stamps.)

After the failure of this experiment I started doing my own research again. A sociologist back home wrote that I should avoid the superficial approach and make a sincere attempt to discover their inner hopes and fears, their secret tragedies.

"Be a big brother to them," he counselled.

Several gallons of cold tea later I found myself one night eyeing the Oriental tootsie on the other side of the gin-rummy deck and clutching my head and sobbing, "If only this cursed rain would stop. Always this rain, rain, rain!"

But anyway, how can you be a Big Brother to somebody who keeps calling you Pops?

NGUYEN CAO-KY — THIRTY-FIVE AND AGING FAST

(October 16, 1965)

SAIGON – Nguyen Cao-Ky, the thirty-five-year-old Prime Minister of South Viet Nam, is said to be an admirer of Napoleon. If so, he must sometimes remember what the fledgling Bonaparte told the Directors of France when they were about to refuse him an important command because he was too young. "In a year I shall be either old or dead."

On October 24, Ky will have completed his fourth month as chief of state. Compared with the five predecessors who had tried and failed with a total of ten governments in just over a year and a half, he is already a veritable Methuselah among post-Diem prime ministers.

His personal image has aged along with his régime. His vigour and flashing good looks have not diminished but their owner appears to be bidding a reluctant farewell to the Ky that used to be – the playboy fighter-pilot who was somehow thrust into politics. Latterly he has been trying to introduce his countrymen, his American allies and – it sometimes seems, himself – to the natural statesman who just happened to have a little fun and adventure on the way to his natural destiny.

A veteran newsman who knew him very well away back when – "when" in this case being any time before last June – says that even in his first month as premier, Ky still reminded him of Cassius Clay. But now, except on the rare occasions when he puts on his famous mauve and black flying suit and allows himself a fling with a fast new U.S. aeroplane, he behaves and looks more like the Anthony Eden of thirty years ago.

It was in the latter role that he made his most recent major public appearance. When he stepped off the plane at Tan Son Nhut airport after his diplomatic visit to Malaysia last week, the guard of honour was there, the band was there, the Cabinet min-

167

isters and military brass were all there in full array – in short everything was ready for the dashing, panoplied entrance that Ky used to love and still presumably does.

He appeared at the doorway of the plane smiling gravely and a little wanly. He was carefully tailored in a conservative black suit, white shirt and pearl-grey morning tie. His second wife, an Air Viet Nam hostess for whom the first Mrs. Ky recently made a tactful Oriental exit, appeared briefly behind him, a stunning vision in turquoise. Then she melted out of sight while the Prime Minister walked slowly past the honour guard, greeted the members of his government and his military commanders and went inside for the press and television interview. There were none of the old friendly wisecracks with the old reporters. His long preliminary statement consisted mainly of statistics on the common problems of Malaysia and South Viet Nam. They were delivered with monumental calm.

To a foreign ear the inflections of spoken Vietnamese can make even a telephone number sound shrill and almost panic-stricken, but Ky had this characteristic tone of excitement in complete subjugation. When he switched into his presentable English he was as solemn and sedative as Lyndon Johnson reading from a teleprompter.

As a performance it was impressive. As a barometer of Ky's prospects of survival it was probably irrelevant, for before the press conference was over, Ky, under persistent prodding, felt obliged to admit that he had just decided to fire another province chief for misappropriation of funds. The day afterward the government was forced to disclose still another major scandal involving some twenty junior army officers and a brigadier-general who had been missing from the country for more than a month along with several million piastres of his other ranks' canteen money. Almost simultaneously a provincial police chief was arrested for extorting huge bribes from black marketeers and draft dodgers. The number of policemen arrested or in hiding for looting the warehouses they were guarding on the Saigon waterfront had meanwhile risen to thirty-five.

Almost every week brings another scandal here that would topple any democratic government overnight and that only a dictatorship kept in office by a major power could survive for long. And as even high officers of Ky's government admit in private, the corruption that gets found out is only the top fifth of one iceberg.

168

The fifth that is discovered becomes another iceberg and only a fifth of that fifth ever comes within the view of the public.

But desperate as they are, the problems of graft and venality have been so long with the Vietnamese that they're not the greatest hazard to Ky's survival. Nor, for similar reasons, are the Viet Cong. Though it has little to do with Ky, the military side of the struggle against the v.c.'s has taken a demonstrable turn for the better. If the premier can't take the credit for the massive increase in u.s. power, at least there's less to blame him for than was the case with his less strongly supported predecessors.

Both these pluses for Ky are essentially negative. And, unhappily, all the minuses that overtook and finally overcame Minh Khanh, and the civilians Oanh, Huong and Quat are still built right into the job.

Ky has yet to win or pacify the quietly troublesome Buddhists or the twenty-five thousand noisier, loosely organized university students of Hue, Saigon and Dalat. Even the chained and censored South Vietnamese press is more inclined to praise him for what he says he's going to do than what he's done already.

Ky is going manfully through the motions of winning the peasants, newly-discovered by both the Americans and the Vietnamese as the most important class of all. But to most Vietnamese villagers and rice farmers, authority – Chinese authority, French authority, Japanese authority, Saigon authority, American authority – has spelled trouble throughout their history and a Prime Minister dropping out of the clouds to shake their hands is not a compelling figure. With peasant perversity they are apt to find themselves closer to the Communist cadres who have lived among them and terrorized them and shared and stolen their rice and made them die and died with them for well over twenty years.

Even Ky's strongest prop, the army, must be considered an uncertain one. The junta meeting that chose him as premier gave him only half as many votes as it gave to Nguyen Chanh Thi, the toughest and most able of the army's four corps commanders.

Thi, perhaps reflecting on the low life expectancy of South Vietnamese Prime Ministers, stepped handsomely aside. But he has remained the most political of all the political generals. He is a prolific, angry speech-maker, runs his own corps areas according to his own mood of the moment and his own *ad hoc* rules, and sometimes announces or explains national policy before Ky himself has had his say.

Both Ky and Thi are dependant ultimately on the loyalty of the young officers' corps to which they themselves belong and which has been the well-spring of the last two years of coups and counter-coups.

Last month, disturbed by civilian criticism of the war and its handling, Ky summoned an armed forces convention in Saigon. Its announced purpose was to discuss "the stand of the armed forces on the problem of national leadership."

Quite clearly Ky – and Thi, who shared top billing with him on the speaker's rostrum – expected the two thousand officers who poured in from the battlefronts to stage a pep rally. In the face of the army's solidarity the Buddhists, the students and the nation's restless older intellectuals could hardly go so far as to forget that this is indeed a military government, and much too tough and united a government for anyone outside it to trifle with. But although the press was barred, even the official news releases could not conceal the fact that the convention developed into a sort of teach-in.

Ky, Thi and other Cabinet members were drawn into what amounted to open debate on everything from "corruption, the system of promotion within the forces, the treatment of soldiers' dependents and the treatment of disabled veterans" to "social justice and social revolution." There was no sign that the armed forces themselves were nearing revolution; nor was there any sign that either Ky or Thi or any of the higher military brass can count on the support of the lower echelons as a matter of course.

In the long run, of course, one source of support – or non-support – will do more to decide Ky's tenure than all the others put together. Without the approval or at least the toleration of the American embassy and the American military command no South Vietnamese premier can hope for even the consolations of honest failure. For now, Ky has the Americans' general acquiescence, if only because the Americans have begun to conclude that almost every new trial in the Vietnamese government automatically brings a new error. He might conceivably last as long as the war itself, which might be a very long time indeed.

Ky's start with the u.s. establishment was not a promising one. He made a point of not applauding when Henry Cabot Lodge was reappointed as ambassador, and when Lodge arrived Ky was out of the country. Lodge, under diplomatic inhibitions, made no comment. But it did not go unnoticed that a few weeks later the ambassador who preceded him, Maxwell Taylor, sighed publicly

170

that he feared the latest premier of South Viet Nam might still not be the right one.

Since then the premier and the ambassador have appeared to be more friendly. But on the day Ky returned from Malaysia, Lodge also happened to be at the airport greeting three visiting U.S. senators. As Lodge strode out to the parking lot and Ky made his measured entrance past the honour guard it was difficult not to notice that the ambassador looked remarkably youthful for a man of sixty-three and the premier looked every day of thirty-five.

WHEN ONE WAR ENDED AND ANOTHER BEGAN

(May 8, 1965)

This is a week of anniversary, the twentieth anniversary of the great Mayday when at last the last Great War ended. It ended with at least fifty-two million people dead and two billion others awakened to the discovery that they still had a chance to live.

It was the kind of day that stole up on people.

In some of the big cities, New York and Toronto and Los Angeles, for instance, they had a chance to turn up the lights and crack out the booze and kiss the girls and have a proper celebration. But in most of the places where the war had been fought, it was a feeble and anti-climactic war's-end. There had been a couple of false armistices by the time they made it official and everybody was pretty tired, uncertain, hungry, bereaved or hurt.

During that long spring there were a number of theoretical endings to the war. I saw one in Paris, another one in Rotterdam, another in Amsterdam and one in Brussels, and several more in sad little villages across the Rhine.

The most dramatic ending I saw occurred at a place called Torgau in East Germany, on the River Elbe. It was there that the official meeting of the Russians and the Americans took place, just as Berlin fell an hour's drive away.

Another reporter and I caught a jeep and raced through the smoldering countryside to be there at the meeting. Sure enough there they were, the Russians on the east bank and the Americans on the west bank.

We went across in a little pontoon boat powered by an outboard motor and were greeted by a Russian colonel with stainless-steel teeth and a platoon of thirty Russian other ranks. About twenty-five American G.I.'s had made their way ahead of us and were there trading watches, shouts, handclasps, friendly punches and outrageous lies about their recent military careers.

Every single one of the Russians had come all the way from Stalingrad, personally and on foot. Every one of the Americans was a veteran of Pearl Harbor or at the very least, Tunisia.

My fellow Canadian and I explained that, for our part, we found the D-Day landings in Italy and Normandy somewhat difficult. Without pressing the matter we dropped a reminder that, whatever could be said in condemnation or explanation of this lunatic war now coming to its end, our little country, Canada, had been in it longer than both their big fat countries put together.

We got along great. The Americans burst into foolish choruses of "Sweet Adeline" and "Down by the Old Mill Stream" and exchanged more watches and kindly punches with the Russians.

The colonel with the stainless-steel teeth produced a small barrel of excellent Caucasian wine and most of the looted carcass of an ox.

"Canadian!" he cried. "Donna Dobbin!"

It turned out he was talking about Deanna Durbin, the well-known child actress from St. Vital, Manitoba. "Very well liked in Russia!" he shouted. "Donna Dobbin is extremely well liked in Russia."

We said that was great, and got on with eating the ox and drinking the wine. It was as pleasant a morning as you ever saw. Very occasionally a random vengeful shell-burst from the totally routed Germans would burst in upon the pleasant riverside and once, in a moment of sheer exuberance, one of the happy Russian soldiers shot one of his friends through the upper clavicle, the wound fortunately proving to be reasonably minor.

"Donna Dobbin!" the colonel with the stainless-steel teeth cried.

"Long live Stalin!" one of the American G.I.'s cried.

"Long live Roosevelt! Long live Churchill!"

There might have been some talk any minute about Mackenzie King. This would have been awkward, for the other Canadian and I never saw eye-to-eye on him.

"Long live Donna Dobbin!" I shouted, to change the subject.

At that precise instant, on that lovely May day on the east bank of the Elbe, the old war ended and the new one began.

The iron curtain – a phrase and a concept not even yet invented – crashed down on that green and lovely riverside like the crashing of an unknown doom.

What happened was that three little Opel staff cars came hurtling down the roadway from the direction of Berlin. A whole ram's-horn of Russian brass spilled forth, lieutenant-generals, major-generals and much worse, a seedy little array of their little political commissars.

In an instant my friend, the colonel with the stainless-steel teeth, the admirer of Roosevelt, Churchill, Deanna Durbin and – if given a little reasonable help with the name, Mackenzie King – became my enemy.

He got to his feet, saluted in terror to the Russian brass, bowed to the commissars, turned his back away from me and the other Canadian and all the suddenly quiet American G.I.'s.

There were new shouts now and they were not happy ones. The Russian G.I.'s moved back from their new friends, the Americans. The colonel with the stainless-steel teeth refused my parting handshake, for it was obvious we were going different ways.

A Russian lieutenant came along while everyone stood abashed, some scared, some just ashamed and desolate. He ordered everybody into the pontoon boats, ordered everybody who wasn't a Russian to get back across the river.

Some of the G.I.'s were indignant and resentful but they were good experienced soldiers so they got in the boats. There were no farewells from their new-found, new-lost friends, for the Russian brass were watching them.

They took us back across the river, a wide serene river at that place, a third of a mile perhaps. When we got there a young American captain, who had been looking over to see what was going on, said, "God damn it, this is crazy!"

So he went over there himself, all alone in the little pontoon boat to go and remind the Russians they were friends. When he was a hundred yards off shore a heavy machine gun was aimed at him and a Russian sergeant was waving him away. When the boat touched the shore another Russian came and kicked the boat off with his foot and the gun was now right down the captain's throat. The young captain was weeping when he got back to the other bank – some might have said with anger or frustration; I'd have said with vanished hope.

A day of so later we got to Berlin. But once more someone had passed on orders from somewhere. When we got through the

Brandenburg gate and the still-smoking ruins of the chancellery beside which Hitler had died, a Russian soldier came out of one of the piles of rubble and stuck a gun in my ribs and still would not look at my papers or listen to my arguments.

Although none of us knew it at the time, the old war was over and the new one had begun.

Perhaps one of the reasons why Ralph Allen was such an unusual human being was that he had the quality of making nearly every man he met think that he alone understood and appreciated the true Ralph, that he was probably the only one who could comprehend what went on under the sometimes puzzling façade Allen presented to the world. Just how this empathy was achieved is hard to analyse since Ralph was never known to have actually said to anybody: Look, you and I understand each other; or even obliquely, you and I are friends. But if you were fat and shy and tongue-tied, he had a way of letting you know that he sometimes felt fat and shy and tongue-tied too. And if you tried in halting or in flowing sentences to let him know you had stumbled in your unusual sensitivity on some truth about existence, he would indicate that truth had hit him too. And if you belonged to the curious *milieu* of the "*real* newspaperman" – that circumscribed world in which men are judged on the basis of a head for liquor, a tendency to zany exploits, and a further talent for droll descriptions of these real or imagined eccentricities – well, he could match you there too.

It was only on further reflection that friends realized it wasn't so much that they had understood Ralph but that Ralph had understood them. After his death, when they tried to articulate what knowing him had meant, they were usually reduced to telling anecdotes that illustrated, more than anything else, the good times they had had in his company.

And Ralph did pursue pleasure with zestful concentration, apparently seeing in fishing, horse-racing, card-playing and curling an antidote to the strains his work and his conscience put on him – a somehow simpler and sunnier existence where the dark side of his nature had no place.

The men he chose to relax with rarely had anything to do with his job (although many of them were in the news business)

175

and they cherished a view of him quite different from that held by his employees. Though they were men with different interests and different ambitions, they had in common a disdain for sham.

In the last twenty years of his life some of Ralph Allen's best days were spent on the fishing trips he set out on regularly every summer, usually in the company of Gillis Purcell of the *Canadian Press,* Gregory Clark of *Weekend Magazine* and Bruce West of *The Globe and Mail,* but occasionally with other companions, including members of the Canadian War Correspondents Association and his own younger son, Gene. The anecdotes told about those holidays could (and probably should) fill a long and funny book.

To realize what kind of fisherman Ralph was, Greg Clark maintained, "you had to know first of all that he was completely anti-mechanical. 'Things' always confounded him; he was forever stepping on his fishing-rods; he never could learn to tie knots; he regarded outboard motors as evil contraptions. But he was almost always a lucky fisherman and even on the bad days, when he had fallen into the water a couple of times, had jammed the outboard half a dozen times and had come home with a miserable catch, he could stop his critics dead with a few quick, crabby and yet beautifully turned sentences, placing the blame squarely, not on Allen, but on everybody (including the Almighty) and everything else."

Part of one extended holiday was spent at McGregor's Bay in Northern Ontario, a legendary fishing-hole where Franklin Roosevelt had done his serious angling. Gil Purcell never forgot a gloomy Sunday there when he and Ralph had an experience, ever afterwards recounted as "the Saga of Doorly Bay."

Early on that rainy afternoon, Purcell and Allen were standing on a small wooden bridge in sight of the big old-fashioned hotel where they were staying, leaning over the railing, fishing idly and sharing a bottle of Doorly's Macaw, a Barbados rum that was a favourite chill-chaser and spirit-raiser. Allen had just taken a swallow, set the corked rum carefully down by his feet and turned back to his rod when he awkwardly, maddeningly, unbelievably, kicked the bottle into the swift water below.

He and Purcell watched it (Oh, lost! the last bottle and on an Ontario Sunday) bobbing out on the current to God knows what oceans beyond for ten horrified seconds, before Allen decided to take action. He loaded a protesting Purcell into a punt, and they labouriously rowed downstream toward the open water, searching every crevice and reed bed until at last they found it, as

Allen had continued to maintain they would, caught in an indent in a rocky outcrop (promptly named Doorly's Bay) and then rowed back again, brandishing the bottle in triumph, singing snatches of the Piper's Lament.

Even Ralph's rages, which occurred often on these trips and weren't always entirely mock, were remembered not with irritation but with laughter. "We'd sit around after a day's fishing, benign with good drink and good food, and talk about life and politics," Greg Clark recalled, "and Allen would listen to us silently for a while and then deliver himself of the opinion – expressed in that wonderfully clear voice which once heard was unforgettable – that we were the most prejudiced men he'd ever encounter, a trio of jackanapes, a flock of fools."

After many of these trips – and many bitter complaints about the quality of the food – Ralph set about to make himself into a master cook, assuming the identity of "Rudolpho the chef," calling crabbily for the host to produce, in small isolated cabins, garlic-presses, lemon-slicers, genuine Hungarian paprika, vintage white wine, and concocting "pickerel almandine à la Rudolpho" or "pork chops Rudolpho" which seemed to those men on those occasions dishes fit for the most fastidious gourmet.

And they probably were too, for everything Ralph did, he did intensely, determined not just to participate but to excel. He bet every horse-race as if his honour depended on winning (though he often lost), and played every bridge game as though a championship was at stake.

Occasionally his natural defects – such as a dismal sense of direction – would down him momentarily but he was never willing to give in to them. When he got lost, as he often did on country roads and city streets, he would claim that it was the directions provided which were in error.

"I remember one night when he was coming to play bridge at my house for maybe the twentieth time," Jack Brunton, a Toronto lumber executive who was Ralph's friend for twenty-five years, was fond of recalling, "and he was half an hour late. He finally arrived, looking pretty sheepish and it came out that he'd managed to mistake a house standing exactly one block north for ours. Nobody answered the door there, so he went inside, hung up his coat, and when the owner came out of the kitchen, Ralph asked him forthrightly (figuring he was the new partner promised for the game), 'Where's the booze?' "

177

To Jack Brunton, and to most of the other men he relaxed with, Ralph never talked about the job he was engrossed in, or the book he was writing, or the discomforts he suffered from the various physical ailments that plagued him. And he never boasted to anyone at any time about his accomplishments or his knowledge so that when you heard him on the radio quiz programme "Now I Ask You," in which he participated for years in the learned company of J. B. McGeachy, Morley Callaghan, and James Bannerman, his easy erudition on a variety of obscure subjects always came as a considerable surprise.

He hardly ever revealed that he was something of a puritan, with a stern (though by no means unforgiving) moral sense. Stu Keate, publisher of the Vancouver *Sun* and a lifetime friend, was surprised once when he and his wife were driving to a dinner party with Ralph to hear him say, when reminded of the film "La Dolce Vita" by a movie marquee on the way, that he had detested it "because there wasn't one person in it that you could say was good."

In many ways he was out of sympathy with the taste of his times. His eldest son, Glen, who had inherited his father's writing talent and his sensitivity, once tried to interest him in J. D. Salinger, and the Young Turks on *Maclean's* tried to convince him that Norman Mailer was a first-rate writer; but he soon put them aside with the remark that Anthony Trollope could outwrite them both.

"It wasn't," as Ken Lefolii once said, "that his opinions were always correct, or even that his logic was always flawless, but his instincts were as right as a man's can be. So you felt, if it's good enough for Ralph to be wrong about, that's good enough for me."

When he died his friends derived what comfort they could from discussing his complexities. His funeral was attended, as he had wanted, only by his family but afterwards, mourners came in unhappy droves to his home to see his wife Birdeen, and his children, Glen, Gail and Gene. His *confrères* from the old days on *Maclean's* gathered to hold a wake at Gerry Anglin's house on the Friday night of his death. At noon that same day one of the most talented – and most rambunctious – of his employees on the *Star* tried to wreck the Toronto Press Club because people were still drinking and laughing in there even though Ralph lay dead. And over the next three or four days, Greg Clark received close to fifty phone calls from people all over the country who "simply needed to talk to somebody about how they felt about Ralph."

Others mourned his loss in public, revealing, as his sister Carroll Dale said, "facets of his character that added new dimensions to my view of him." Jim Coleman wrote in the Toronto *Telegram,* "How strange that I of all people should have been chosen to know a great man." And Ken Lefolii said simply and eloquently on the CBC, "He was the best man I've known." And Colin McDougall, of McGill University, (whose novel Ralph had published in *Maclean's*) wrote, "He was a man who stood in sunlight and brought warmth to those around him."

Ralph Allen wouldn't have liked these tributes (or any of the dozens of others which were published) very much; at least, they would have caused his face to flush, his jaw to work and his eyes to go opaque under his glasses. But that was part of why he was such a great editor and such a good man – and part of why we loved him.

ACKNOWLEDGEMENTS

This book owes its existence to the generous help and warm encouragement given by Ralph Allen's family, friends and colleagues. I would particularly like to express gratitude to the following who, either in published material or in personal interviews, provided assessments of Ralph Allen's achievements, insights into his character and reminiscences of his exploits.

Birdeen Allen
Glen Allen
Pierre Berton
Jack Brunton
June Callwood
Gregory Clark
Jim Coleman
Carroll Dale
Vern De Geer
Milt Dunnell
Robert Fulford
Trent Frayne
Sydney Halter
Beland Honderich

Stuart Keate
W. Arthur Irwin
Vince Leah
Ken Lefolii
Charles Lynch
Cam MacKenzie
Ben Malkin
Ross Munro
Gillis Purcell
Maurice Smith
Joan Weatherseed
Bruce West
Laurie Wilgin
Scott Young

CMCN

The following is a list of the articles used in this book and their sources. Where there is a difference between the title used in *The Man from Oxbow* and the title under which the article first appeared in the newspaper or magazine, the original title is listed in parenthesis.

FROM *THE GLOBE AND MAIL*

Sports Scribe Insulted (Sports Scribe Insulted, Burglar Greets Arrival) *December, 1938*

Mostly Incidental *December, 1941*

The Sarge Steps out *April, 1943*

Easter Bells *May, 1943*

Churchill in the Commons (Churchill Electrifies Commons) *June, 1943*

The Caves, the Villas, the Kitchens of Italy (War Correspondents Have Housing Problem) *September, 1943*

Italian Massacre (21 Forced to Kneel before Firing Squad) *September, 1943*

Press Conference *March, 1944*

Sleepless and Hungry Canadians Slug Ahead *June, 1944*

Twilight of Youth *June, 1944*

The French and their Invaders (French Teach Patience to their Invaders) *August, 1944*

Notable Sights and Sounds in a War-filled Country *August, 1944*

A Black and Thunderous Nightmare: Canadians Bombed by 500 RAF Planes (Canadians Bombed by 500 RAF Planes) *August, 1944*

Normandy Tales *August, 1944*

The Liberation of Paris (City Wild With Joy) *August, 1944*

French vs. Patois *September, 1944*

Capitals Compared *September, 1944*

By-passed Magic *September, 1944*

Why Don't the Huns Surrender? *March, 1945*

Deceptive Spring *March, 1945*

Trek to the Rhine (Ragged Civilians Leave Razed Rhineland Town) *March, 1945*

Gotterdammerung (Nazis Die like Animals as Doom Grips Town) *April, 1945*